# WORKBOOK

WorldView

4

## SERIES EDITOR: MICHAEL ROST

## Karen Davy

Longman

**WorldView Workbook 4**

Authorized adaptation from the United Kingdom edition entitled *Language to Go*, First Edition, published by Pearson Education Limited publishing under its Longman imprint. Copyright © 2002 by Pearson Education Limited

American English adaptation published by Pearson Education, Inc. Copyright © 2005.

Pearson Education, 10 Bank Street, White Plains, NY 10606

Editorial director: Pamela Fishman
Development director: Irene Frankel
Senior development editor: José Antonio Méndez
Vice president, director of design and production: Rhea Banker
Executive managing editor: Linda Moser
Associate managing editor: Mike Kemper
Production editor: Sasha Kintzler
Art director: Elizabeth Carlson
Vice president, director of international marketing: Bruno Paul
Senior manufacturing buyer: Edie Pullman
Text and cover design: Elizabeth Carlson
Photo research: Aerin Csigay
Text composition: Word & Image Design

ISBN-10: 0-13-184017-7
ISBN-13: 978-0-13-184017-1
Printed in the United States of America
10 11 12 13 14–V011–17 16 15 14 13

**Acknowledgments**
Contributing writer Wendy Long, for her work on the Self-Quizzes; Ellen Shaw and Pamela Vittorio, for their work on the Readings.

**Ilustration Credits**
Steve Attoe, pages 4-11, 30, 67, 103, 131; Pierre Berthiaume, 44, 66, 84, 115; Brian Hughes, 24, 40, 92, 122; Paul McCusker, 16, 20, 98; Suzanne Mogensen, 13, 48, 52, 75, 76, 97; Steve Schulman, 60, 71, 112; Neil Stewart, 27, 33, 105.

**Photo credits**
Page 15 John R. Jones/Papilio/Corbis; 17 (left) Jan Butchofsky-Houser/Corbis, (right) Kevin Schafer/Getty Images; 19 Jeff Hunter/Getty Images; 27 Ryan McVay/Getty Images; 35 Tim Hall/Getty Images; 37 Reuters/Corbis; 45 Spencer Grant/PhotoEdit; 51 Uli Wiesmeier/Getty Images; 55 (left) Alan Schein Photography/Corbis, (right) Joe Sohm/Chromosohm/ Stock Connection/ PictureQuest; 63 Ian McKinnell/Getty Images; 68 Kingfisher Challenges; 69 Bettmann/Corbis; 72 (top) Thinkstock/Getty Images, (bottom) Ray Kachatorian /Getty Images; 73 Layne Kennedy/Corbis; 79 Carlo Allegri/Getty Images; 80 Agency France Presse; 85 The Photographers Library; 90 Jurgen Schadeberg; 94 Photofest; 107 Royalty-Free/Corbis; 108 GoGo Images/Glow Images; 109 Digital Vision/Getty Images; 123 Kim Kulish/Corbis; 126 Donna Day/Getty Images; 129 Chris Baker/Getty Images.

# Contents

# Learning Strategies

## Listening Strategies
Here are 6 ways to improve your listening.

Check (✓) the strategies that you use now. Try a new strategy each week. In the column on the right, write the date you tried it and take notes about your experience. Did the strategy help you learn?

**1** ☐ **Find new sources**

What do you like to listen to or watch in English? Movies? Songs? News broadcasts? TV shows? The radio? Interviews? Conversations? Find some new sources for listening. Try the radio, TV, CDs, DVDs, the Internet, your computer lab, or someplace where you can hear people speak English. Listen at least one hour a week.

**Try this now:**

What do you like to listen to in English? (songs, movies, etc.) Write two or three ideas.

What are your favorite sources for listening to English? (CDs, Internet, etc.) Write two or three sources.

Date: _____

Notes: _____

_____

_____

_____

_____

_____

_____

**2** ☐ **Listen for a specific purpose**

When you listen, you don't need to understand everything. Listen for a specific purpose. What information do you want to find out? Names, numbers, important events, key information, the speaker's attitude, or the main idea?

**Try this now:**

Think about some different listening situations. What listening purpose would you have in each of these?

• You're at an airport. There's an announcement.
• You're driving in your car. There's a song on the radio.
• You're at home. There's a news broadcast on TV.

Date: _____

Notes: _____

_____

_____

_____

_____

_____

_____

**3** ☐ **Take notes and reconstruct ideas**

Taking notes is helpful when you need to remember important ideas or facts, for example, when you listen to a lecture or watch a documentary. When you take notes, write down key words and main ideas in the order you hear them. After you have finished listening, go back to your notes right away. "Reconstruct" your notes—rebuild the ideas from the notes you have made. Say or write out complete sentences. Or if possible, go over your notes out loud with a classmate.

**Try this now:**

Look at notes you have taken recently while listening to a lecture or a documentary. (Or listen to a recording now and take new notes.) For each key expression in your notes, say a full sentence to express an idea.

Date: _____

Notes: _____

_____

_____

_____

_____

_____

_____

## 4 ☐ Respond as you listen

Responding is an important part of interactive listening. There are different ways to respond. If you don't understand something, ask a clarification question, such as *What does _____ mean?* If you want to learn more, ask an information question, such as *Who did ...? When was...? Why will...?* To show the speaker that you're paying attention, use a feedback phrase, such as *Uh-huh* or *I see*. And to participate further, give a personal response, such as *That's great* or *I'm sorry to hear that*.

**Try this now:**

Here are some responses you can make when you are listening. Label each one: (CQ) clarification question, (IQ) Information question, (FP) feedback phrase, or (PR) personal response.

Oh? _____    Why did you do that? _____

What do you mean? _____    Did you say "yesterday"? _____

Ah-hah! _____    Sounds nice. _____    No way! _____

Mm-hmm. _____    Hmm? _____    That's strange! _____

Yeah. I think so, too. _____    I'm not so sure about that. _____

Date: _____

Notes: _____

Date: _____

Notes: _____

_____

_____

_____

_____

_____

_____

## 5 ☐ Listen and memorize

When we have interesting tapes, CDs, or sound files, we can develop our "listening memory" if we listen more than one time. Choose a song with English lyrics. Listen to the song several times. Each time, try to memorize more of the lyrics. You can write them or repeat them in your mind. You can also do this with recorded conversations, poems, speeches, or stories.

**Try this now:**

Write the names of two of your favorite English language songs, poems, or stories that you want to memorize.

Date: _____

Notes: _____

_____

_____

_____

_____

_____

_____

## 6 ☐ Keep a listening notebook

Keep a record of your listening experiences. After you listen to a news broadcast or watch a movie, write for three minutes in your listening notebook. Write a summary or a reaction or some new vocabulary or expressions. Write in your notebook at least twice a week.

**Try this now:**

Think about some ideas for your listening notebook. Which might be helpful for you to write? Write a plus (+) sign.

_____ a summary          _____ new expressions

_____ questions          _____ impressions

_____ other notes _____

Date: _____

Notes: _____

_____

_____

_____

_____

_____

_____

_____

# Learning Strategies

## Vocabulary Strategies

Here are 6 ways to increase your vocabulary.

Check (✓) the strategies that you use now. Try a new strategy each week. In the column on the right, write the date you tried it and take notes about your experience. Did the strategy help you learn?

**1** ☐ **Add "shared" words to your vocabulary**

What English words are similar in your language? For example, *optimist* in English and *optimista* in Spanish are very similar. Think of "shared" words between English and your language. (Most languages have hundreds of shared words.)

**Try this now:**

How do you say these English words in your language? Which ones are shared words in English? Do they have the same meaning?

*color   data   favor   information   tourist*

What other shared words do you know?

Date: _____

Notes: _____

_____

_____

_____

_____

_____

_____

**2** ☐ **Make word webs**

Make word webs to show how words are related. Each line is a new link for the word.

Make one word web each week in a vocabulary notebook. Save the word webs and add new words to them.

**Try this now:**

Make a word web for two of these words. Add about 5 links for each one.

*clutter   grow up   achieve   prison   popular*

Date: _____

Notes: _____

_____

_____

_____

_____

_____

_____

**3** ☐ **Learn word "affixes"**

You can expand your vocabulary if you learn to build word families. One way to do this is by using word "affixes—prefixes and suffixes added to a word root to change its meaning. When you learn a new word, find out about "related" words that will expand the meaning of the word.

Some common prefixes are:
- a-, ab-, il-, im-, in-, ir-, un-  (meaning, *not* or *without*)
- co-, col-, com-, con-, cor- (meaning, *with* or *together*)

Some common suffixes are:
- -able, -ible (meaning, *having the quality of, capable of*)
- -ify, -ize (meaning, *give a particular quality*)

**Try this now:**

Look at the words below. Identify the prefix or suffix in each word. What does the word mean? Do you know any other words in each "family"?

*immobile   rationalize   indestructible   appearance*

Date: _____

Notes: _____

_____

_____

_____

_____

_____

_____

## 4 ☐ Narrate in English

Look around you or watch a video with no sound, or take a walk outside. As you look, say what you see in English. You can say the names of objects (for example, *a tree, a red car, a man with a hat, a clear blue sky*) or you can describe actions (for example, *a child is talking to her mother*). Say at least 15 things. Try this once a week for 5 minutes.

**Try this now:**

Look around you now. Name at least 15 things you see, in English. Then say something about each thing. (Example: *My cell phone also works as a digital camera.*) Does this help you "think in English"?

Date: _____

Notes: _____
_____
_____
_____
_____
_____
_____

## 5 ☐ Use a memory technique

Use a memory technique to help you remember new words. One method is the "key word method." It is a way of mixing sounds and images. For a new word, think of an image, using ideas from your language or from English. For example, *executive* is a *businessperson who makes decisions for the business*. The first part sounds like "eggs" and the third part sounds like "cute", so you might picture a businessman at a desk with three "cute" eggs above his head. He is trying to decide which one to choose. This mixed image may help you remember the new word.

**Try this now:**

Think about memory techniques you use. Find the meaning of these English words and try to memorize them using the "key word method" or another memory technique.

*morose*      *frazzled*      *can't stand*

Date: _____

Notes: _____
_____
_____
_____
_____
_____
_____

## 6 ☐ Use your dictionary actively

Bilingual dictionaries are useful for finding a quick translation of an English word. However, if you use a *monolingual* dictionary, you can learn a lot about the words, such as the different meanings of the word, the usage of the word, and related words. This information will help you remember the word and use it more accurately. Use a good dictionary and look up at least five unfamiliar words every day.

**Try this now:**

Look up three of these words in a monolingual dictionary, for example, try the *Longman Dictionary of American English*. Find out as much as you can about each word.

| | | |
|---|---|---|
| promontory | backlash | relegate |
| staccato | ambiguous | effervescent |

Date: _____

Notes: _____
_____
_____
_____
_____
_____
_____

# Learning Strategies

## Speaking Strategies

Here are 6 ways to improve your speaking.

Check (✓) the strategies that you use now. Try a new strategy each week. In the column on the right, write the date you tried it and take notes about your experience. Did the strategy help you learn?

**1** ☐ **Get feedback from a conversation partner**

Find a conversation partner. Meet at least once a week for 30 minutes. Speak English only and help each other. Make a note of any of your grammar mistakes that your conversation partner (or your English teacher or classmates) notices.

**Try this now:**

Find a conversation partner if you don't have one. Meet regularly to speak in English.

Date: _____

Notes: _____

_____

_____

_____

_____

_____

**2** ☐ **Say it in different words**

When you are in a conversation, paraphrase the main points that your partner says. Say the ideas in your own words (*You mean...?*). If you practice saying the same idea quickly in different ways, you will improve your conversation fluency.

**Try this now:**

Say and write a paraphrase for each sentence.

1. We're going to the beach tomorrow unless it rains. (Start with *You mean you won't...*).

2. We have to go to the store to get more food for the party. (Start with *Are you saying that we don't...*)

3. Can you give me your cell phone number in case I need to call you tonight? (Start with *Oh, so you...*)

Date: _____

Notes: _____

_____

_____

_____

_____

_____

**3** ☐ **Rehearse the conversation**

Choose a topic to talk about informally in English, such as your job, a movie you've just seen, or something funny that happened. Write short notes (not sentences!) on a card. Now record your speech (try not to look at your card). Picture your audience. Talk for two minutes. Then play back your speech and compare it with the transcript. What can you improve by changing the grammar or words? The next day, don't look at your transcript and record the same speech. This time, try to say your ideas in one minute.

**Try this now:**

Imagine you are giving a short speech to your class. Try these topics for a short speech:

• a childhood memory
• someone who has influenced me
• (another topic): _____

Date: _____

Notes: _____

_____

_____

_____

_____

_____

**4** ☐ **Make a list of target phrases**

Make a list of target phrases, the phrases that have difficult sounds for you. Put these on notes and post them around your home, on the refrigerator, on your mirror, etc. Practice saying your target phrases every day—loudly, clearly and confidently. If you wish, practice in front of a mirror (to watch your face muscles and lips).

**Try this now:**

Which of these phrases contain sounds that are difficult for you to pronounce?

a few drops of olive oil        six sticks of butter
a chunk of cheese              rice and shrimp

What other English sounds, names, words, or phrases are difficult for you to pronounce? Make a list.

Date: _____

Notes: _____

_____

_____

_____

_____

_____

_____

_____

**5** ☐ **Speak in phrases**

When fluent speakers speak English, they connect words, and the sounds in the words are linked together. There are many phrases in English that have linked sounds, such as *wanna* for *want to* and *gonna* for *going to.*

**Try this now:**

The underlined spellings here show how the phrases are pronounced. First, rewrite the phrase with its normal spelling. Then pronounce it with the linked sounds.

*Howzit* going?        *Howja* like the movie?
*Whaddaya* think?      *Whatser* name?
*C'mon.* Hurry up.     *Seeya* later.
I *hafta* go home.     I *wanna* talk to you.
I've *gotta* go.       *G'won.* I'll be there in a minute.

What other phrases with linked sounds do you know?

Date: _____

Notes: _____

_____

_____

_____

_____

_____

_____

**6** ☐ **Find your own voice**

Choose a story, like a children's story or part of a novel. Record yourself on audio or video three times. Each time, set a goal to improve one specific area of your pronunciation: loudness and clarity, chunking (saying words in groups), prominence (stressing the most important word in each chunk), intonation (making your pitch rise and fall clearly), or individual sounds. Listen to your recording. Note where you have improved your pronunciation.

**Try this now:**

Think about some stories or books in English from which you can read aloud. What are two you can use to make a recording (a specific story or part of a story)?

_____

_____

Date: _____

Notes: _____

_____

_____

_____

_____

_____

# Learning Strategies

## Reading Strategies

**Here are 6 ways to improve your reading.**

Check (✓) the strategies that you use now. Try a new strategy each week. In the column on the right, write the date you tried it and take notes about your experience. Did the strategy help you learn?

**1** ☐ **Read for pleasure**

The most effective way to improve your reading ability is by "reading for pleasure." Find a book that is comfortable for you to read. ("Comfortable" means that you can understand about 90% of the words.) Read in English about topics you are interested in. Use popular books or translations of books you've read in your native language. Read every day for 30 minutes or more.

**Try this now:**

What kinds of books do you like most (science fiction, romance novels, adventure stories, historical novels, etc.)?

What are some books you'd like to read in English?

Date: _____

Notes: _____

_____

_____

_____

_____

_____

_____

**2** ☐ **"Pre-read" first**

You can improve your concentration when you read if you "pre-read" an article first. Skim over the article quickly. Look at the headings. Predict some ideas in the reading. Now read just the first line of each paragraph. Think about what you know about the topics in the article. After you "pre-read" the article quickly in this way, you will know the "gist"—the main idea—of the article. Then go back and read more carefully.

**Try this now:**

Find a long article in an English newspaper or magazine. Pre-read the article for one minute. Did pre-reading help you read the article more effectively?

Date: _____

Notes: _____

_____

_____

_____

_____

_____

_____

**3** ☐ **Read with a purpose**

When you read a chapter in a textbook or a short article, it's important to focus and read with a specific purpose. Before you read, think of two or three things you want to find out and write these down. As you read, stop from time to time to think about your purpose. Don't worry about parts of the text that don't help you with your reading purpose.

**Try this now:**

Choose a reading passage from your *WorldView Student Book* or from a news magazine. Before you read, write three questions you want to answer as you read. Now read the passage. Did the questions help you focus as you read?

Date: _____

Notes: _____

_____

_____

_____

_____

_____

**4** □ **Guess new words from context**

*confused*
*bewildered*

When you read in your second language, there will always be some unfamiliar words. In order to be a fluent reader, it is important to guess the meaning of new words from context. If you look at the surrounding sentence or paragraph, you can often think of a paraphrase of the unfamiliar word. By guessing new words from context, you will increase your reading fluency.

**Try this now:**

Guess the meaning of the "words" in bold below (they're not really words in English). What context clues did you use to guess the meaning?

• Mary and Alan seemed happily married, but I knew their relationship was actually **incanbivalent**.

• Max was finally promoted to **anbruster** of the art department after 20 years of being a design assistant.

• After a few minutes of **cygnactic** conversation with Iris, I realized I hadn't heard a word she was saying.

Date: _____

Notes: _____

_____

_____

_____

_____

_____

_____

**5** □ **Read critically**

When you read news or opinion articles, it is important to read critically—to evaluate the facts, the ideas, and the writer's point of view. Are the facts clear? Is anything missing that you need to know? Are the ideas logical? What is the writer's point of view? What other points of view are possible? What is your response to the writer's ideas?

**Try this now:**

Choose an "opinion article" from a newspaper or news magazine or news website. Read the article. As you read, answer these critical reading questions: Are the facts clear and complete? Is the writer's point of view "fair"? What other points of view are possible?

Date: _____

Notes: _____

_____

_____

_____

_____

_____

_____

**6** □ **Apply what you read**

If you want to remember what you read, do something while you are reading and after you finish reading. For example, while you read, you can take notes or make an outline. After you read, you can reflect on the reading, in a notebook or in an audio (tape) journal. Write or say a short summary. Talk about the things you are reading about.

**Try this now:**

Which of these ideas will you use in your reading this week?

__ read and take notes
__ write a summary or report after I have finished reading
__ write out an inspirational passage from a book
__ start an audio journal
__ make notes of new vocabulary or concepts
__ talk about what I am reading
__ form a reading group

Date: _____

Notes: _____

_____

_____

_____

_____

_____

_____

11

# UNIT 1

# Changes

## Vocabulary

**1** Label the situations with words from the box. You will not use all the words.

| | | | |
|---|---|---|---|
| clutter | contentment | energy | good health |
| luck | happiness | productivity | ~~stress~~ |
| success | tension | tranquility | wealth |

1. Angela and Phil don't have a minute to relax. Their three children require constant attention. _____ *stress* _____

2. Alex's room is full of papers, books, newspapers, clothes, and sports equipment. I don't know how he finds anything in that mess! _____

3. Martha is never sick. She hasn't missed a single day at work for the entire year. _____

4. Many professional athletes receive millions of dollars a year and even more from companies whose products they advertise. _____

5. Ralph applied to five schools. He expects to hear from them this week. He's really worried. _____

6. Marlene gets a lot of work done every day. Every morning, she writes down her goals for the day and doesn't go home until she's crossed everything off her list. _____

7. Taku won a one-week vacation in Paris in a radio contest. The prize was for the thirteenth person to call, and that was her! _____

8. Karen gets up at six in the morning, exercises for an hour, and then goes to work. In the evening, she cooks dinner, does a little housework, and helps her children with their homework. She should be exhausted, but she never feels tired. _____

9. The sea breeze and the sound of the waves make the remote beach at the end of the island an ideal place to relax and clear my head. _____

10. Ron's first novel became an instant bestseller, and it is being translated into three languages. _____

**2** Write the adjectives that describe the people or situations in Exercise 1.

1. _____ *stressful* _____     6. _____

2. _____     7. _____

3. _____     8. _____

4. _____     9. _____

5. _____     10. _____

# Grammar

**3** Complete the conversations with *yet, already,* or *just*.

**1. A:** Has Julia cleaned her room ____yet____?

   **B:** Well, she's almost done. She has picked up the clutter _____ , but she hasn't taken out the trash _____ .

**2. A:** Have you tried the burgers at Scotty's _____?

   **B:** No, and I probably won't. You obviously don't know this, but I've _____ become a vegetarian, so I've given up meat.

**3. A:** Have you heard the news _____? The company has laid off almost 100 employees.

   **B:** Yes, I heard about it and I've _____ started working on my resume. We should be prepared for anything.

**4. A:** Do you have a minute? I've _____ made an important decision, and I'm anxious to talk about it. I haven't told anyone about it _____. I've asked Felicia to marry me, and she said yes!

**4** Write two sentences about each picture. Use the present perfect of the verbs and *yet, already,* or *just* in each sentence.

**1.** Amanda / sign up / at a gym
She / not start / exercising

Amanda has just signed up at a gym.
She hasn't started exercising yet.

**2.** Phil / walk / Skippy / three times today
They / take / their evening walk

**3.** Cesar buy / the paper
He / not read / it

**4.** Matt / complain / to his neighbors many times
They / not stop / making noise

**5.** Kim / get / a raise
She / receive / three raises this year

**6.** Justin / have / breakfast
He / not get / ready for work

# 1

## Listening 🔊

**5** 🎧 **Play track 2. Listen to the interview with Bill Costa. Check (✓) the Feng Shui ideas he has tried.**

Bill Costa has . . .

started to exercise. ✓

started having a glass of water in the morning. _____

recently bought goldfish. _____

changed his eating habits. _____

decorated his home and workplace with plants. _____

started wearing blue clothes. _____

started to avoid crowded streets and noisy traffic. _____

**6** 🎧 **Play track 2 again. Which sentence do you hear? Listen and circle *a* or *b*.**

**1. a.** Bill Costa, a computer analyst from San Francisco, has agreed to try out some of the ideas behind Feng Shui.

   **b.** Bill Costa, a computer analyst from San Francisco, agreed to try out some of the ideas behind Feng Shui.

**2. a.** I've already started running every morning.

   **b.** I've just started running every morning.

**3. a.** I don't think Feng Shui really changed my life much.

   **b.** I don't think Feng Shui has really changed my life much.

**4. a.** I've already owned a couple of goldfish.

   **b.** I already owned a couple of goldfish.

**5. a.** They've never brought me much luck.

   **b.** They never brought me much luck.

**6. a.** It's really helped me concentrate better.

   **b.** It's really helping me concentrate better.

## Pronunciation 🔊

**7** 🎧 **Play track 3. Notice how the intonation changes on the focus word. Underline the focus word in each sentence.**

**1.** Has your life <u>changed</u> yet?

**2.** What changes have you made in your life?

**3.** Have you bought any fish yet?

**4.** How about straightening up your workplace?

**8** 🎧 **Play track 3 again. Listen and repeat.**

## Reading

**9** Read the title of the article. Which of the following do you think will be discussed?

a. How some people age quickly

b. How some people get healthier as they age

c. How some people stay young

**10** Read the article. Which statement do you think best represents the author's beliefs?

a. Lifestyle is as important as diet, air, and water in aging "youthfully."

b. It is hard to know whether it is lifestyle, or diet, air, and water which is more important in the process of aging "youthfully."

c. Diet, air, and water are more important than lifestyle in the process of aging "youthfully."

# GROWING old youthfully

Have you ever thought about what it means to get old? It's a time when many people develop health problems, when their hair turns gray, when their skin becomes **wrinkled**, and when they start to lose their hearing, sight, and the ability to think clearly. But what if it were possible to age chronologically while remaining healthy and youthful?

There are a few communities around the world; for example, the Vilcabambas of Ecuador, the Hunza of Pakistan, and the Abkhazians of Georgia, that seem to have succeeded in doing just that. It is not uncommon for people in these communities to live productive, active lives beyond the age of one hundred. What is the key to their **longevity**?

One important factor seems to be location. All three of these communities are situated at high **elevations** in remote places. Because of the **harsh** living conditions they have to endure, these people are expected to help one another and share with one another. Family **ties** are particularly strong, and crime is **rare**. These people seem to live relatively stress-free, tranquil lives in harmony with nature and with one another.

Of course, a stress-free life isn't the only reason they live so long; a nutritious diet, pure air, and glacial water are critical, as well. In addition, in all of these places there is a strong sense of prestige in aging. The elderly are respected, and their experience in life is valued, so they continue to contribute to the community, even in their old age.

**11** Read the article again. Underline the correct word to complete each sentence.

1. The communities described in the article are **far from / near** other communities.

2. These communities are **near the ocean / in the mountains**.

3. According to the article, people from **warm / cold** places are more likely to live longer.

4. People in these communities take care of one another because they **love / need** one another.

**12** Find the word in bold that means

a. connections _____  b. not smooth _____  c. difficult _____

# Australia

## Vocabulary

**1** In the "word snake" below, there are eight compound nouns for travel items. Circle the words.

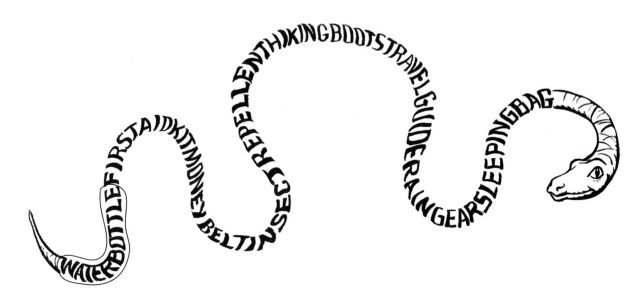

**2** Complete the sentences with the words from Exercise 1.

1. When you travel, it can be dangerous to keep your cash and credit card in your pocket. Instead, you should use a _money belt_ .

2. You can't wear sneakers on these trails. Where are the _____ you bought last week?

3. Don't forget your _____. It's supposed to rain all weekend.

4. Look at all the mosquitoes. We'd better put on some _____ , or they'll eat us alive.

5. The _____ recommends this restaurant, but I don't like the looks of it. Let's go somewhere else.

6. Lou fell and cut his finger. It doesn't look serious, but we'll need the _____ to take care of it.

7. I'm really thirsty. Have you seen my _____?

8. This _____ is almost as comfortable and warm as my bed at home.

## Grammar 🔊

**3** A talk show host is talking to a travel expert about Ecuador and the Galapagos Islands. Complete the conditional sentences with the present tense or the future of the verbs in parentheses. Use contractions when possible.

**Host:** So what should we know if we ___want___ to visit Ecuador?
1. (want)

**Expert:** First of all, if you _____ nature, you _____ an amazing experience
2. (enjoy)  3. (have)

in Ecuador. If you _____ in the capital city of Quito, you _____
4. (land)  5. (be)

less than a day's drive from the Amazon jungle, a snow-covered active volcano,

or a tropical beach.

**Host:** And when is the best time to go to Ecuador?

**Expert:** Unless crowds _____ you, don't go December through January or
6. (not bother)

June through August. February through May are the best months to visit Ecuador.

**Host:** And what about the Galapagos Islands? I've heard they're awesome.

**Expert:** If you _____ on a very tight budget, you shouldn't miss a visit to the
7. (not be)

Galapagos Islands. The Galapagos are one of the world's greatest natural treasures.

If you _____ the trip, it _____ cheap. But it _____ worth the
8. (make)  9. (not be)  10. ( be)

expense if you _____ to go.
11. (decide)

**Host:** And what can visitors see on the islands?

**Expert:** If you _____ , you _____ an amazing variety of plant and animal life.
12. (go)  13. (see)

Unless you _____ very unlucky, you _____ sight of animals such as sea
14. (be)  15. (catch)

lions, penguins, turtles, and whales.

**Host:** Whales? Wow! OK. If you _____ , we _____ phone calls now from
16. (not mind)  17. (take)

our viewers.

**Expert:** No, I don't mind at all.

**Host:** If you _____ questions or comments for our expert, call us now at the studio.
18. (have)

## 2

## Listening 🎧

**4** 🎧 Play track 5. Listen to the conversation between Jeff and his roommate. Check (✓) the thing(s) Jeff will take on the trip.

sleeping bag ___✓___          rain gear _____

hiking boots _____            sunscreen _____

insect repellent _____        travel guide _____

**5** 🎧 Play track 5 again. Complete the sentences.

**1.** Jeff is going to spend the weekend _____.

    **a.** with his roommate

    **b.** at the beach

    **c.** in the mountains

**2.** According to Jeff's roommate, the _____ are the worst in the evening.

    **a.** birds

    **b.** bears

    **c.** bugs

**3.** Jeff doesn't want his roommate's rain gear because _____.

    **a.** he's already packed his own

    **b.** it's probably going to be a dry weekend

    **c.** he likes rainy weather

**4.** Jeff's roommate <u>doesn't</u> warn him about _____.

    **a.** sunburn

    **b.** wild animals

    **c.** insects

## Pronunciation 🎧

**6** 🎧 Play track 4. Listen. Underline the parts of the words that are stressed.

**1.** first-<u>aid</u> kit

**2.** hiking boots

**3.** insect repellent

**4.** money belt

**5.** rain gear

**6.** sleeping bag

**7.** travel guide

**8.** water bottle

**7** 🎧 Play track 4 again. Listen and repeat.

# Reading

**8** Guess. What is the Great Barrier Reef made of?

a. fish          b. seaweed          c. coral          d. sea turtles

**9** Read the article. Which of the following would be another title for this section of a guidebook?
a. An Unusual Underwater Forest
b. A Dangerous Place for Ships
c. How Unique Animals Live Together

# The Great Barrier Reef

The Great Barrier Reef, located off the northeastern coast of Australia, is the ideal destination for both the adventurous and the nature-loving traveler. The Reef is made up of thousands of **tiny** marine animals called corals. These sea creatures join together to form larger groups, or reefs, which look like small underwater forests. At nearly 31,000 square kilometers wide, marine biologists call the reef "the largest living structure created by sea **organisms**." It is so large that it can be seen by astronauts from space.

In addition to the 400 different types of corals that live on the ocean floor, the reef is home to 1,500 kinds of tropical fish, beautiful varieties of seaweed, and six different types of sea turtles. Dolphins, whales, and even sharks swim in the waters above the reef. The Great Barrier Reef is also the final resting place of thirty historic shipwrecks, including the **ill-fated** *HMS Pandora* of 1791, now a famous archaeological site and a popular stop for anyone interested in underwater exploration.

Visitors interested in a close view of the Reef and its fascinating and colorful inhabitants can snorkel or go scuba-diving in some of the Reef's designated areas. Not-so-adventurous travelers who prefer not getting wet—or who would rather avoid an **up-close** encounter with some of the Reef's **inhabitants**—may prefer a guided tour on the popular glass-bottom boats. Passengers can see nearly sixty meters in depth as the boats sail over the clear turquoise waters.

**10** Read the article again. Write *T* (true) or *F* (false) after each statement about the Great Barrier Reef.

1. It can most probably be seen from an airplane. _____

2. Divers are allowed to go wherever they want there. _____

3. Most of the shipwrecks were moved to a museum. _____

**11** Find the word in bold that means

a. unlucky _____          b. residents _____          c. small _____

# UNIT 3

# What's cooking?

## Vocabulary

**1** Write the words for the pictures. What's the word in the box?

1. <u>b  a  s  i  l</u>
2. __ __ __ __ __
3. __ __ __ __ __
4. __ __ __ __ __
5. __ __ __ __ __ __ __
6. __ __ __ __ __ __ __ __
7. __ __ __ __ __ __
8. __ __ __ __ __ __
9. __ __ __ __ __ __ __ __ __
10. __ __ __ __ __
11. __ __ __ __ __

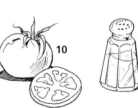

**2** Complete the cooking instructions with the appropriate form of the verbs in the box.

| boil | ~~broil~~ | chop | melt | pour | sauté | serve | simmer | stir |
|------|-----------|------|------|------|-------|-------|--------|------|

1. _Broil_ the fish for two minutes on each side.
2. Heat the cheese until it _____.
3. _____ the sauce over the fish.
4. _____ the carrots into small pieces.
5. _____ the mushrooms in a little butter.
6. Turn down the heat and allow the sauce to _____ for ten minutes.
7. _____ the pasta for 15 minutes in a large pot.
8. _____ the pasta frequently with a wooden spoon.
9. Spoon the fish and sauce over the pasta and _____ hot.

20

# Grammar 🔊

**3** Read the ingredient list. Then choose the correct words to complete the conversation.

---

## *Pasta with broccoli and potatoes*

| | |
|---|---|
| 2 potatoes | ¾ teaspoon salt |
| 4 cups broccoli florets | ½ teaspoon pepper |
| 2 tablespoons olive oil | 1 pound pasta |
| 1 onion | ⅓ cup grated cheese |
| 4 cloves garlic | |

---

**A:** What are you doing?

**B:** I'm making a list. I've decided to try a new recipe tonight, and I have to go out and get some of the ingredients.

**A:** What are you going to make?

**B:** It's called pasta with broccoli and potatoes, and it sounds delicious.

**A:** Do you need **(1) a lot of / a great deal of** things?

**B:** Not **(2) too many / too much**. We already have **(3) most of / much of** them. The recipe calls for **(4) a few / a little** potatoes and **(5) several / a little** cups of broccoli florets. And **(6) a few / a little** chopped onion and **(7) plenty of / a number of** minced garlic.

**A:** Is that all?

**B:** Well, no. I'll need **(8) a little / a few** salt and pepper, but we have that, of course. I also need **(9) a little bit of / a small number of** oil. Do we have any?

**A:** There **(10) aren't many / isn't much** oil left, so you'd better get some.

**B:** OK. And I need **(11) some / all** pasta and **(12) a little / a few** grated cheese.

**4** Use the phrases in the box to change the underlined expressions so that they mean the opposite.

| | | | | |
|---|---|---|---|---|
| a great deal of | a large number of | a little | few | ~~not many~~ |

1. Some experts say <u>most of</u> us eat well. *Some experts say not many of us eat well.*

2. We should eat <u>a little</u> fruit every week. _____

3. <u>Hardly any of</u> these recipes sound good. _____

4. Too <u>many</u> people worry about their diets. _____

5. There's <u>a lot of</u> food left over from the party. _____

# 3

## Listening 🔊

**5** 🎧 Play track 6. Listen to the first recipe (chili con carne) from Chef Le Blanc. Number the recipe steps in the correct order.

_____ Chop the garlic.

_1_ Put the kidney beans in water and boil them.

_____ Bring the chili con carne to a boil and let it simmer.

_____ Heat some of the oil.

_____ Add the seasonings—garlic, salt, pepper, chili powder.

_____ Serve with rice.

_____ Add the ground beef.

_____ Simmer the beans for about 30 minutes.

_____ Simmer the chili con carne for 30 minutes.

_____ Add the onions.

_____ Sauté the beef.

_____ Add the tomato paste, chopped tomatoes, and kidney beans.

**6** 🎧 Play track 6 again. Correct the underlined word or phrase in each statement about the recipe for chili con carne.

a little bit of

**1.** Next, we heat ~~some~~ oil in another saucepan.

**2.** Not <u>a lot of</u> oil, because we don't want it to be greasy.

**3.** We <u>simmer</u> these until the beef turns brown.

**4.** Not <u>a lot</u> because, you see, this chili powder is very, very hot.

## Pronunciation 🔊

**7** 🎧 Play track 7. Notice how some words in the sentence are not stressed. Listen and fill in the blanks to complete the sentences.

**1.** Chop _____ clove _____ garlic.

**2.** Heat _____ oil _____ _____ pan.

**3.** Add _____ little salt _____ pepper.

**4.** Don't use _____ _____ _____ chili pepper.

**8** 🎧 Play track 7 again. Listen and repeat.

22

# Reading

**9** **Which do you think is the most popular food in the U.S.?**

chili con carne _____    hamburgers _____    hot dogs _____    ice cream _____    pizza _____

**10** **Read the article. Which is the best title for it?**

**a.** Fast Food History      **b.** The German Hamburger      **c.** The History of the Hamburger

The hamburger is undoubtedly the most popular American food of all time, surpassing hot dogs, ice cream, and even pizza. People in the U.S. consume about 38 billion burgers annually, both at home and in restaurants. Placed end to end, the line of hamburgers would reach nearly 2 million miles.

Some say the hamburger originated in Germany, where a popular dish was ground beef, cooked lightly with onions. In the early nineteenth century, immigrants from Hamburg, Germany, brought this dish to the U.S., where it was popularized as "Hamburg style steak." This was not yet the handheld hamburger sandwich in a bun, though it may have been a **forerunner**.

No one knows exactly when the modern hamburger was invented, but the most widely reported "first appearance" was at the 1904 World's Fair in St. Louis, Missouri, where cooked patties of ground beef were served on bread rolls. Mass distribution of hamburgers began in the 1920s with the White Castle company: with three stores, it became the first hamburger restaurant **chain**. Hamburgers cost five cents each, and the company's **slogan** was "Buy 'em by the sack." Bob's Big Boy, Wimpy, and other hamburger chains followed, but none has ever reached the success of McDonald's, the world's biggest chain. The number of burgers sold to date by McDonald's is twelve times the world's population.

In **fancy** restaurants you might find gourmet burgers served with less **conventional** toppings, such as guacamole, chili, or goat cheese. But, by far, the most popular condiments are ketchup, mustard, onions, pickles, and mayonnaise. And to complete the meal, a side of fries and a Coke® are a must.

**11** **Read the article again. Write _T_ (true) or _F_ (false) after each statement.**

**1.** People have eaten hamburger sandwiches since the early nineteenth century. _____

**2.** McDonald's was the first company to sell hamburgers. _____

**3.** Guacamole is a common side dish to accompany a hamburger. _____

**12** **Find the word in bold that means**

**a.** a group of stores or restaurants _____    **b.** elegant _____    **c.** predecessor _____

# Toys of the future

## Vocabulary ◖▬▬

**1** What are the people talking about? Match the statements with the toys and games in the box.

| | | |
|---|---|---|
| **a.** action figure | **b.** board game | **c.** cards |
| **d.** doll | **e.** ~~erector set truck~~ | **f.** handheld video game |
| **g.** remote-controlled car | **h.** skateboard | **i.** stuffed animal |

1. "When I was a kid, I used to build things like that. Once I made a sports car and a robot." __e__

2. "Oh, look at those teddy bears. Aren't they cute? Maybe I'll get one for Marnie's baby." _____

3. "Those guys are really strong. If I get one, I can pretend he's a hero who's going to save the world." _____

4. "If Mom and Dad buy me that beautiful one with black hair, I'll name her Sarah and make her pretty dresses." _____

5. "Do you think I could have one of those for my birthday? My friend Leo could teach me how to ride it." _____

6. "I'd love to have one of those. It's so small that it would fit in my pocket, so I could play with it on the school bus." _____

7. "I'm going to buy a deck so that I can do a few tricks that I learned from my cousin. These tricks are amazing—you'll think I can read your mind!" _____

8. "With some of those, the whole family could play in the evening instead of watching TV all the time. Monopoly™ and Scrabble™ are two of my favorites." _____

9. "I saw a girl in the park with one of those the other day. It went really far, and then it came back to her." _____

**2** Which toys and games in Exercise 1 . . .

a. represent a person or an animal? _action figure_ _____ _____

b. have wheels? _____ _____ _____

c. have win-or-lose results? _____ _____ _____

# Grammar

**3** Use *will*, *may*, *might*, or *could* to rewrite the sentences so that they have the same meaning. Some items can be rewritten in more than one way.

1. In the future, children will possibly have very little time to play.

   *In the future, children might have very little time to play.*

2. I don't know if toys will change much in the future.

   _____

3. It's possible that most children will play video games.

   _____

4. It's possible that kids will spend less time watching TV.

   _____

5. I think it's very likely that children are going to spend a lot of time surfing the Internet.

   _____

**4** Find the eight mistakes with verbs in this letter to a newspaper editor and correct them. The first mistake has been corrected for you. There may be more than one way to correct some of the mistakes.

Something has been bothering me, and I've decided to let you know about it. I doubt if you

~~could~~ will like my letter, but I'm sure many people who read your newspaper may agree with me.

The paper might not wants to print my letter because I have some pretty negative things to say,

but I have to say them.

Last Sunday you had a special section called "Toys Our Children Won't to Be Able to Live

Without." You showed pictures of video games and other expensive toys that many parents

like me cannot to afford. The article said that children who don't have these toys could

having trouble in school. The toy companies claim their products can help children be better

learners. I don't think having or not having a certain toy won't affect a child in school. But it

will causes a child to be unhappy or upset if he or she doesn't have the same toy everyone

else has. Kids are only human! Please don't publish anything in the future that will hurt our

children. Thank you.

# 4

## Listening

**5** Play track 8. Listen to the radio interview with a sociologist about the future of toys. The interviewer and the sociologist express different opinions. Read each statement and decide whose opinion it expresses. Write *I* (Interviewer) or *S* (Sociologist).

1. "Children won't know what's real and what's not real." __I__

2. "Shy children will benefit from playing with an animated, or virtual, child." _____

3. "Having children interact with toys will prevent them from trying to make real friends." _____

4. "It makes me uncomfortable to think about toys that could know when a child is unhappy." _____

5. "Virtual friends might be better than real friends." _____

6. "It's strange to think about a child whose best friend is a machine." _____

**6** Play track 8 again. Complete the sentences with the words you hear.

1. I'm sure they _____, and it _____ happen sooner than we think.

2. So children _____ _____ even know what's real?

3. That _____ happen.

4. I think some children, especially shy or lonely ones, _____ want a virtual friend.

5. You know, we _____ also see "emotionally sensitive" toys.

6. Some children _____ find that their virtual friends understand them better than their real friends!

## Pronunciation

**7** Play track 9. Notice the way the focus words (the most important words) in each sentence stand out. Underline the focus words.

1. I'm <u>sure</u> little girls will play with <u>dolls</u>.

2. I expect they'll have discussions with their dolls.

3. Do you really think dolls will talk to people?

4. I'm sure they will.

5. Do you think this could happen any time soon?

6. It might happen sooner than we think.

**8** Play track 9 again. Listen and repeat.

## Reading

**9** Read the title of the article. What do you think is the writer's opinion of video games?

    **a.** They are too violent.    **b.** They might cause violent behavior.

**10** Read the article. What is the main idea?
    **a.** Violent video games should not be available to children.
    **b.** The relationship between violence in video games and real life is not clear.
    **d.** Video games don't cause violent behavior because people can distinguish between games and reality.

# VIDEO GAMES AND VIOLENCE

When people think about video games, they often think about violence. There has long been a concern that virtual violence in video games leads to actual violence in the real world. Is this concern justified?

Many people fear that children will associate the excitement they get from shooting a video **villain** with the feeling they might get from hurting someone in real life. Numerous scientific studies **claim** that playing violent video games can increase a person's aggressive thoughts and feelings. Researchers also argue that violent video games are more **harmful** than violent television shows and movies because video games are interactive and players become so involved in them, and the games often require the player to play the role of the violent aggressor.

However, defenders of video games do not accept the validity of such research. They claim that the research was done in laboratories in which real **aggression** was not permitted, so scientists had to measure "pretend" aggression. These scientists did not take into account that video-game players understand the difference between real and simulated violence, and if they were asked to commit actual violent acts after playing a violent game, the **vast** majority would refuse. Video-game fans feel that violent video games do not cause violence; they only **reflect** the violence already in our world.

As any video-game player knows, the visual quality of video-games is advancing rapidly. As video game violence becomes more and more realistic, we can only hope that the relationship between video games and violence will be more fully understood soon.

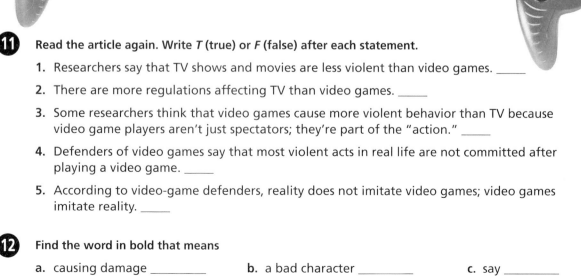

**11** Read the article again. Write *T* (true) or *F* (false) after each statement.

    **1.** Researchers say that TV shows and movies are less violent than video games. _____

    **2.** There are more regulations affecting TV than video games. _____

    **3.** Some researchers think that video games cause more violent behavior than TV because video game players aren't just spectators; they're part of the "action." _____

    **4.** Defenders of video games say that most violent acts in real life are not committed after playing a video game. _____

    **5.** According to video-game defenders, reality does not imitate video games; video games imitate reality. _____

**12** Find the word in bold that means

    **a.** causing damage _____    **b.** a bad character _____    **c.** say _____

# Self-Quiz for Units 1–4

## Vocabulary

### UNIT 1

**A**  Read each pair of words. Write *S* if the words have the same or nearly the same meaning. Write *O* if they have opposite meanings.

1. clutter        empty space     _O_
2. relaxation      stress        ____
3. wealth        a lot of money     ____
4. contentment      happiness     ____
5. tranquillity      tension     ____
6. success        a bad result     ____

### UNIT 2

**B**  Match the words on the left to their uses.

1. money belt _f_      **a.** Use this to avoid mosquito bites.
2. insect repellent _____      **b.** Use this if you don't want to get wet.
3. travel guide _____      **c.** Use this if you want to carry something to drink.
4. rain gear _____      **d.** Use this to learn about a place.
5. first-aid kit _____      **e.** Use this if you get hurt.
6. water bottle _____      **f.** Use this to carry small things that you don't want to lose.

### UNIT 3

**C**  Circle the food that goes with each verb.

1. melt      (butter)      kidney beans
2. chop      onions      stock
3. pour      beer      tomatoes
4. sauté      garlic      chili powder
5. simmer      water      ground beef
6. broil      shrimp      pepper

### UNIT 4

**D**  Use a word from the box to complete each sentence.

| | | |
|---|---|---|
| action figure | cards | handheld video game |
| jigsaw puzzle | skateboard | ~~stuffed animal~~ |

1. This __stuffed animal__ looks like a real cat.
2. Timmy went outside to ride his _____.
3. When you put together the pieces of a _____ , it makes a picture.
4. You can play many different games with _____ , but it's a good idea not to play for money.
5. Carrie played her _____ in the car.
6. The toy company based this _____ on a character from a famous movie.

28

# Grammar

## UNIT 1

**A** Complete the sentences with *already*, *just*, or *yet*.

1. Jessica is not taking the paper with her because she's read it _already_ .

2. I've _____ finished my report and I'm about to make copies.

3. We need an answer soon. Has the director called _____?

4. If she's _____ eaten her vegetables, then she can have a cookie.

5. The snow hasn't melted _____ even though it has been sunny.

6. He's tried five diets _____ , but none seems to work.

## UNIT 2

**B** Complete the sentences with the appropriate form of the verbs in parentheses.

1. You _'ll like____ **(like)** Squaw Peak if you enjoy hiking.

2. If you _____ **(travel)** in January, the hotels will be less crowded.

3. If the plane _____ **(be)** late, we'll need something to read.

4. Unless you _____ **(like)** cold weather, avoid December through March.

5. They _____ **(be)** safer if they take a first-aid kit.

6. If you _____ **(buy)** tickets early, you can save money.

## UNIT 3

**C** Cross out the quantifier that does **not** go with each food in bold.

| 1. basil | ~~a few~~ | a little | plenty of |
|---|---|---|---|
| 2. tomato paste | many | not much | a lot of |
| 3. onions | a little | a lot of | a great deal of |
| 4. chili powder | a lot of | some | several |
| 5. chicken stock | many | a large amount of | a little bit of |
| 6. oil | all | plenty of | some |

## UNIT 4

**D** Complete the sentences with *will*, *may*, *might*, or *could*. Write all possible answers.

1. We feel very confident. We think the group __will___ finish the project on time.

2. That toy isn't popular now, but it _____ be popular in the future. We hope it is.

3. In 20 years, people _____ have cars that fly. No one knows for sure.

4. I haven't finished the book. The characters _____ fall in love at the end.

5. I'm sure the children _____ like the candy.

6. Her new job is at a TV station, and she _____ meet famous people. Who knows?

# How rude!

## Vocabulary

**1** Match the verbs on the left with the phrases on the right to form expressions related to table manners. One verb goes with two phrases.

**1.** point ___b___     **a.** your nose

**2.** reach _____     **b.** at someone

**3.** blow _____     **c.** your feet up on the chair

**4.** snap _____     **d.** with your fingers

**5.** slurp _____     **e.** while drinking

**6.** put _____     **f.** your elbows on the table

**7.** eat _____     **g.** across the table

　　　　　　　**h.** your fingers

**2** Complete the conversations with the appropriate form of the expressions in Exercise 1.

**1. A:** Someone told me it's rude to _put your elbows on the table_ .

　　**B:** Hmm, I'm not sure about that. How could you eat a good sandwich without resting your arms that way?

**2. A:** Sorry I'm _____ my coffee. It's really hot!

　　**B:** Oh, that doesn't bother me a bit. Enjoy it!

**3. A:** I know you've been standing all day and you're tired, but please don't _____. You'll get the cushion dirty.

　　**B:** You're right. Sorry.

**4. A:** Could I please have some silverware?

　　**B:** You don't need a fork and knife to eat fried chicken. Just _____.

**5. A:** Do you have a cold?

　　**B:** Yes, I do. Please excuse me for a minute. I need to go to the restroom to _____.

**6. A:** What's going on over there?

　　**B:** Oh, children can be so cruel. That little boy spilled his soda, and the other kids _____ and laughing.

**7. A:** Is it OK if I _____ so that the waiter hears me and comes to the table?

　　**B:** No. That's rude here. Just hold up your hand and he'll see you.

**8. A:** Marianne, please don't _____. If you want something, ask for it.

　　**B:** Sorry, Mom. Could you please pass the salt?

# Grammar

**3** Put the words in the correct order to write questions asking for permission. Use the appropriate form of the verbs in parentheses.

1. (go out) / tonight / may / please / I

   <u>May I go out tonight, please?</u>  OR  <u>May I please go out tonight?</u>

2. if / OK / we / your lawnmower / (borrow) / is / it

   _____

3. mind / I / do / (turn down) / you / the / if / the TV

   _____

4. you / a phone call / would / if / I / mind / (make)

   _____

5. could / please / (have) / a glass of water / I

   _____

**4** Jessica and Teresa are roommates. Read the situations. Write conversations using the cues.

1. Teresa doesn't have time to wash her breakfast dishes before class. She wants to know if she can leave her dishes in the sink and wash them later. Jessica thinks that's fine.

   T: **(could)** <u>Could I leave my dishes in the sink and wash them later?</u>

   J: _____

2. Jessica has a date tonight, and she wants to borrow Teresa's new green sweater. Teresa has a date, too, and she's planning to wear her new sweater.

   J: **(OK)** _____

   T: _____

3. Teresa has an important exam tomorrow, and she has trouble studying when the TV is on. Jessica would like to watch TV. It's OK with Teresa because she can go to another room to study.

   J: **(do/mind)** _____

   T: _____

4. Jessica wants to invite some friends over on Saturday night. Teresa thinks it's a great idea, and she'd like to have some of her own friends over, too.

   J: **(would/mind)** _____

   T: _____

# 5

## Listening

**5**  🎧 Play track 10. Listen to the conversations and complete the sentences with the correct choice.

**Conversation A**

1. It's OK for the woman to ___*b*___ .
   a. use the phone          b. use the fax machine

**Conversation B**

2. The customer _____ having dinner alone.
   a. is                    b. isn't

**Conversation C**

3. The two women _____ each going to pay half the cost of the meal.
   a. are                   b. aren't

**Conversation D**

4. The people are probably _____ .
   a. in someone's home     b. in a public place

**6**  🎧 Play track 10 again. Which sentence do you hear? Circle *a* or *b*.

1. a. Well, is it OK if I use the fax?
   b. Well, do you mind if I use the fax?

2. a. Sure. Why not?
   b. Sure. Go ahead.

3. a. Waiter, may we have the check, please?
   b. Waiter, can we have the check, please?

4. a. Do you mind if I smoke?
   b. Would you mind if I smoked?

## Pronunciation

**7**  🎧 Play track 11. Notice the intonation in these polite requests. Where does the speaker's voice go down? Mark the word with a falling arrow (⤵). Where does the speaker's voice go up? Mark the word with a rising arrow (⤴).

1. May we have the  check, please?

2. Is it OK if I leave early?

3. Do you mind if I come in?

4. Would you mind if I asked you a question?

**8**  🎧 Play track 11 again. Listen and repeat.

# Reading

**9** Look at the title of the article. Which of these topics do you think will be included?

gift giving _____ greetings _____ table manners _____ weather _____

**10** Read the article. What is the main idea?

a. Many people are impolite.

b. Standards of politeness can vary.

c. People in Rome are the most polite.

d. Eating habits differ throughout the world.

## Polite customs around the world

A famous **saying** goes: "When in Rome, do as the Romans do." It means that when you visit a new place, you should follow the local customs: **Notice** when people greet each other with a **bow**, a handshake, or a kiss; observe how they use their eating utensils; note what they give (or don't give) as gifts.

Here are some examples of customs in different places:

- People in Arab countries eat with the right hand because the left hand is considered unclean.
- In many Asian countries, it is impolite to **expose** the soles of the shoes when sitting down.
- In Brazil, people avoid giving gifts that are purple or black, the colors of **mourning**.
- In China, gifts are offered and taken with two hands.
- In the Dominican Republic, customers clap their hands to ask for the check in a restaurant.
- In Guatemala, it is polite to speak in a soft voice.
- It is polite to **remove** your shoes before entering someone's home in Japan.
- In New Zealand, it is considered rude to chew gum in public.
- In South Korea, younger people remove their eyeglasses when talking to older people, out of respect.
- If someone belches after a meal in Taiwan, it is a compliment to the cook.
- In Thailand, it is very rude to touch someone's head.
- In Japan, it is rude to place your chopsticks across your rice bowl.
- In the Netherlands, people use a knife and fork to eat fruit, cheese, sandwiches, or pizza. It is impolite to use your fingers to eat these foods.
- In the U.S., it is rude to ask someone how much he or she earns.

Which customs are true in your country? Which ones seem strange to you?

**11** Read the article again. In which places are these actions impolite?

1. giving a gift with one hand _____

2. wearing your outside shoes in the house _____

3. chewing gum in public _____

4. eating with your left hand _____

**12** What should or shouldn't you do if . . .

1. you want the check in a restaurant in the Dominican Republic?

2. you want to select a gift for someone in Brazil?

3. you enjoyed your meal at someone's home in Taiwan?

**13** Find the word in bold that means

a. a time of sadness after someone's death _____ b. show _____ c. an incline _____

# UNIT 6

# Achievement

## Vocabulary

**1** Complete the crossword puzzle.

### Across

**3** When the great tennis player Pete Sampras ___achieved___ all his goals, he retired from the sport and never played another professional match.

**5** Electric cars will _____ many of the world's energy problems, but we probably won't see many on the road anytime soon. No one has figured out a way to make them affordable.

**6** Head Start is a U.S. government program that helps preschool children _____ reading, vocabulary, and language skills.

### Down

**1** United Nations secretary-general Kofi Annan _____ the 2000 Nobel Peace Prize for his efforts to help achieve world peace.

**2** Oprah Winfrey _____ the obstacles of racism and sexism, and became the first woman and the first black person to be hired as a news anchor in Nashville, Tennessee.

**4** Before someone can become a lawyer in the U.S., they must _____ a very challenging test called the Bar Exam.

**7** When American actor Adrien Brody _____ his first Academy Award in 2003, he became the youngest Oscar winner for best actor.

# Grammar

**②** **Read each statement. Then answer the question. Circle _Y_ (yes) or _N_ (no).**

1. We've been working in the yard since early this morning, and we're hot and dirty.

   • Are they probably still working in the yard?      (Y)    N

2. The Johnsons have painted their house bright yellow. It used to be blue.

   • Is the house still blue?      Y    N

3. The Costas have been working hard on their house, too, and it looks great!

   • Did they finish fixing up their house?      Y    N

4. He's studied English for many years.

   • Is he still a student?      Y    N

5. He's been studying English for many years.

   • Is he still a student?      Y    N

**③** **Roger is at a job interview. Complete the conversation. Use the present perfect or the present perfect continuous of the verbs in parentheses. In some cases, both forms are correct.**

**Roger:**    I **(1)** _'ve been waiting_ **(wait)** for my
_(thinking)_    interview for almost an hour, and I'm a
     nervous wreck!

**Receptionist:**    Excuse me, Mr. Nello. Mr. Carter is available
     now. He **(2)** _____ **(ask)** me to
     show you to his office. This way, please.

**Mr. Carter:**    Mr. Nello, I'm so sorry you **(3)** _____
     **(have to)** wait for so long, but I **(4)** _____ **(have)** a number of
     emergencies this morning. Thank you for your patience. Now, I **(5)**
     _____ **(look at)** your resumé and I see that you graduated from
     college last year. What **(6)** _____ **(do)** since you finished school?

**Roger:**    I **(7)** _____ **(work)** at my father's store. I help him out as much as
     I can. And of course I **(8)** _____ **(look for)** a "real" job.

**Mr. Carter:**    So you **(9)** _____ **(not work)** in an office since this job you had in
     high school.

**Roger:**    That's right. I had a part-time job at Cohen and Cohen when I was a senior.
     I **(10)** _____ **(not have)** any additional office experience since then,
     but of course I **(11)** _____ **(use)** a computer throughout my college
     career, and I handle a lot of phone orders for my father.

**Mr. Carter:**    That's great. Now, tell me . . .

# 6

## Listening 🔈

**4** 🎧 Play track 14. Listen to the radio program. Write *T* (true) or *F* (false) after each statement. Then correct the false statements. There may be more than one way to correct some sentences.

1. Trevor Baylis is different from most inventors. _____

2. Trevor is a shy, quiet man. _____

3. He came up with the idea for his radio because many people in Africa can't afford expensive radios. _____

4. Trevor took a long time to develop a working model for his radio. _____

5. After his inventions won prizes, Trevor stopped working on new projects. _____

6. At least one of Trevor's inventions may be popular with teenagers. _____

**5** 🎧 Play track 14 again. Check (✓) the correct column in the chart for each device.

| Name of device | Trevor has invented it. | Trevor has been developing it. |
|---|---|---|
| wind-up radio | | |
| wind-up flashlight | | |
| wind-up computer | | |
| wind-up power device | | |
| wind-up in-line skates | | |

## Pronunciation 🔈

**6** 🎧 Play track 15. Notice the pronunciation of the weak and contracted forms of *have* and *has*. Fill in the blanks. Use contractions when possible.

1. Trevor _____ _____ several prizes.

2. He _____ _____ many wind-up devices.

3. What else _____ _____ _____?

4. He _____ _____ _____ on a device that creates electricity.

5. What _____ _____ _____ _____ on?

6. I _____ _____ _____ a new computer game.

**7** 🎧 Play track 15 again. Listen and repeat.

# Reading

**8** Read the quote at the beginning of the article. What do you think it means?
- **a.** Do what you think is right, regardless of other people's opinions.
- **b.** When you think you can achieve a goal, just do it, even if others disagree.
- **c.** Stay away from people who give you bad advice.

**9** Read the article. Why is running Marla's passion?
- **a.** She is not interested in other sports.
- **b.** She feels normal when she runs.
- **c.** She can't see well enough to do other sports.

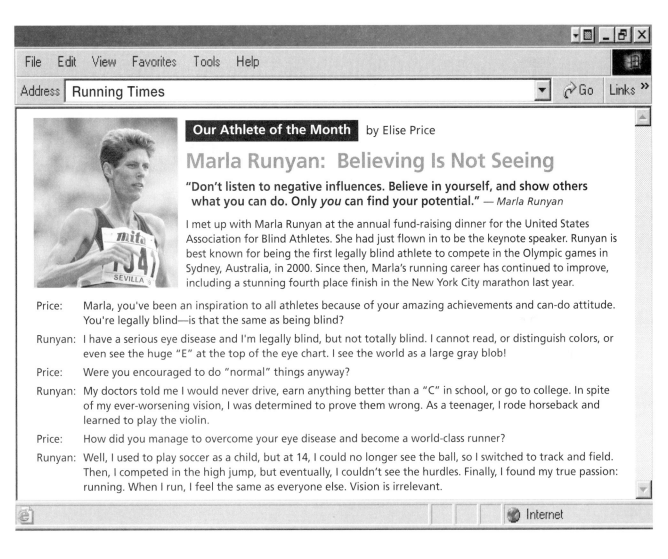

**File  Edit  View  Favorites  Tools  Help**

Address  Running Times          Go   Links »

**Our Athlete of the Month**  by Elise Price

## Marla Runyan:  Believing Is Not Seeing

*"Don't listen to negative influences. Believe in yourself, and show others what you can do. Only you can find your potential."* — Marla Runyan

I met up with Marla Runyan at the annual fund-raising dinner for the United States Association for Blind Athletes. She had just flown in to be the keynote speaker. Runyan is best known for being the first legally blind athlete to compete in the Olympic games in Sydney, Australia, in 2000. Since then, Marla's running career has continued to improve, including a stunning fourth place finish in the New York City marathon last year.

Price:    Marla, you've been an inspiration to all athletes because of your amazing achievements and can-do attitude. You're legally blind—is that the same as being blind?

Runyan:  I have a serious eye disease and I'm legally blind, but not totally blind. I cannot read, or distinguish colors, or even see the huge "E" at the top of the eye chart. I see the world as a large gray blob!

Price:    Were you encouraged to do "normal" things anyway?

Runyan:  My doctors told me I would never drive, earn anything better than a "C" in school, or go to college. In spite of my ever-worsening vision, I was determined to prove them wrong. As a teenager, I rode horseback and learned to play the violin.

Price:    How did you manage to overcome your eye disease and become a world-class runner?

Runyan:  Well, I used to play soccer as a child, but at 14, I could no longer see the ball, so I switched to track and field. Then, I competed in the high jump, but eventually, I couldn't see the hurdles. Finally, I found my true passion: running. When I run, I feel the same as everyone else. Vision is irrelevant.

Internet

**10** Read the article again. Write *T* (true) or *F* (false) after each statement about Marla Runyan.

1. She can distinguish bright colors only. _____

2. When she was a child, the doctors told her that she could lead a normal life. _____

3. She has been an inspiration to other athletes. _____

**11** Find the phrase in the article that means

a feeling that goals are achievable _____

# UNIT 7 Corporate spying

## Vocabulary

**1** Look at the box and find six words or expressions that go with the phrase *a crime* and six that go with the phrase *a criminal*. (Use one word with both.) Write them in the word webs.

| | | | |
|---|---|---|---|
| accuse someone of | check on | commit | convict someone of |
| deter | eavesdrop on | get away with | keep an eye on |
| keep tabs on | spy on | uncover | |

accuse someone of

a crime

**1.**

a criminal

**2.**

**2** Look again at the first word web in Exercise 1. Which means . . .

1. "do something illegal"?                                           *commit a crime*

2. "say someone has done something illegal"?            _____

3. "prove that someone is guilty of a crime in a court of law"?  _____

4. "not be punished for something wrong"?                 _____

5. "discover something secret or hidden"?                  _____

6. "make someone not do something illegal"?             _____

# Grammar

**3** Complete Detective Travis's notes with *to, so that, in case,* and *for*.

Luckily, I remembered to bring my cell phone (1) __in case__ I need to call for backup. I have

to stay far behind this guy (2) _____ he won't see me. My spy camera would be

helpful (3) _____ taking pictures, but I left it at the station. I probably should go

back (4) _____ get it, but I don't want to lose this guy.

**4** Rewrite the sentences in Jason's email so that they have the same meaning. Use the words in parentheses and make any necessary changes.

To: **Kelly**
From: **Jason**
Subject: **Something incredible**

1. I'm writing because I need to tell you something incredible. **(to)**
   I'm writing to tell you something incredible.

2. I'm writing from home because I want to keep this confidential. **(in order to)**
   _____

3. I found out today they've installed a microphone in my office because they want to eavesdrop on me. **(so that)**
   _____

4. The company spies on employees because they need to protect company secrets. **(in order to)**
   _____

5. They also keep an eye on us because they want to make sure we're being productive. **(to)**
   _____

6. I'm being careful with what I say to my co-workers because they might be spies. **(in case)**
   _____

7. The company has installed software to check employees' internet activity. **(for)**
   _____

8. I restrict my email and Internet activities to business purposes because my company might be using surveillance. **(in case)**
   _____

9. I bring my cell phone to work to make personal calls. **(for)**
   _____

# 7

## Listening

**5** ∩ Play track 16. Number the security devices in the order the representative mentions them.

_____ a.

_1_ b.

_____ c.

_____ d.

**6** Match the devices in Exercise 5 with these sentences. Some devices may go with more than one sentence.

1. This doesn't record. _dummy camera (c)_

2. They'd need too many of these. _____

3. People would put them in their pockets. _____

4. The executive likes this one. _____

5. This might create a bad atmosphere in the company. _____

**7** ∩ Play track 16 again. Fill in the blanks.

1. I wanted to meet with you personally _____ show you some of our latest products.

2. I'm wondering if we should invest in some sort of surveillance _____ find out who's responsible.

3. We'd need to buy hundreds of them _____ monitor all our employees.

4. They can be connected to a recorder _____ you'll have evidence _____ you need it later on.

## Pronunciation

**8** Read the words aloud and underline the syllable with the main stress in each word.

1. pro blems
2. install
3. technology
4. criminal
5. solutions

6. responsible
7. suspect (noun)
8. suspect (verb)
9. surveillance
10. security

**9** ∩ Play track 66. Check your answers in Exercise 8.

**10** ∩ Play track 66 again. Listen and repeat.

## Reading 🔊

**11** **Look at the title of the newspaper editorial. Which do you think the author is concerned about?**
**a.** too much surveillance  **b.** not enough security

**12** **Read the article. What is the main idea?**
**a.** There is no freedom without security.
**b.** Businesses have the right to use security devices.
**c.** Our privacy is being threatened by technology.

# Has Surveillance Gone Too Far in the Name of Security?

Did you know that every time you use a credit card or withdraw money from an ATM, you leave a digital **trail** that can be used to access information about you? And smile when you use an ATM because a **surveillance** camera is snapping your picture. Security is a necessity in today's world, but haven't we gone overboard in spying on each other? Security and surveillance devices are putting our privacy, and ultimately our freedom, at risk.

Security cameras monitor parking lots, stores, and other buildings. As if this weren't enough surveillance, cameras monitor intersections, parks, and sidewalks, often disguised as ornaments on buildings. Travel reservations you make, publications you subscribe to, Internet sites you visit—all of these are electronically recorded in a computer somewhere.

What happens to all this information? Most people don't even know it's being collected, let alone how it will be used. Insurance companies, prospective employers, financial institutions, and governments could gain access to private information about you, without your **consent** or knowledge. Of course, this means that computer hackers can also obtain information about you.

Businesses claim they have a right to protect themselves from employee **theft**, shoplifters, and other criminals. Governments say that security is their number one responsibility. Both are right, of course, but is surveillance out of control? If our privacy is threatened, our freedom is in **jeopardy**, too.

**13** **Read the article again and complete the statements.**

1. Five common activities that leave a "digital trail" of someone's identity are _____, _____, _____, _____, and _____.

2. According to the editorial, businesses use surveillance to _____. _____.

3. The author is worried about losing _____.

**14** **Find the word in bold that means**
**a.** permission _____  **b.** danger _____  **c.** trace _____

# UNIT 8

# Up in the air

## Vocabulary ▬▬

**1** Use the words in the box to say where at the airport you might hear someone say the following.

| | | |
|---|---|---|
| ~~baggage claim~~ | gate | runway |
| security checkpoint | check-in counter | duty-free shops |

1. "Has everything come off the plane? My suitcase isn't here." _baggage claim_

2. "The prices aren't so great here. This perfume is cheaper at the drugstore near my house." _____

3. "Sir, please remove your shoes and take everything out of your pockets." _____

4. "Folks, this is your pilot speaking. There are a few planes ahead of us, but we should be cleared for takeoff in five or six minutes." _____

5. "Good morning. We are now ready to board Flight 877. At this time, we invite passengers with small children and passengers with special needs to board first."

_____

6. "So, you're checking one suitcase, and you have one carry-on bag. Here's your boarding pass. Please go to Gate 33." _____

**2** Unscramble the letters to make words related to travel and airports. Then write the words next to the correct definitions.

glifth tatntaden _____ _____

ugeaggl _____

arcry-no gab _____ _____

drabigno spas _____ _____

1. You can't get on the plane without this _____

2. Another word for *baggage* _____

3. A small piece of baggage you take with you on the plane _____

4. The person responsible for passengers' safety and comfort _____

42

# Grammar

**3** Read the clauses. Number the events (a–d) in the correct order to make two sentences.

**1.** a. I decided to take a taxi _____

b. I realized that I had missed the bus _____

c. so, after I had waited 40 minutes for the next one _____

d. when I got to the bus stop ___1___

**2.** a. that the train had just left _____

b. when I looked at my watch I realized _____

c. the train wasn't there _____

d. when I arrived at the station _____

**4** Complete the story with the correct form of the simple past or the past perfect of the verbs in parentheses.

When I **(1)** _reached_ (reach) into my pocket, I **(2)** _____ (realize) I **(3)** _____ (leave) my keys at the office. Fortunately, a few weeks earlier, I **(4)** _____ (give) my upstairs neighbor, Clare, my extra set of keys—in case this ever **(5)** _____ (happen). I **(6)** _____ (run) upstairs and **(7)** _____ (ring) Clare's doorbell, but she **(8)** _____ (not get) home yet. What was I going to do? I **(9)** _____ (need) to get to the airport in two hours, and I **(10)** _____ (not pack) yet. I **(11)** _____ (already decide) to go back to the office to get my keys when Clare **(12)** _____ (step) out of the elevator. I **(13)** _____ (never be) so happy to see someone as I was to see her!

An hour later, I **(14)** _____ (throw) some things into a suitcase and **(15)** _____ (be) on my way to the airport. By the time the taxi **(16)** _____ (drop) me in front of the terminal, I **(17)** _____ (start) to relax. That **(18)** _____ (change) soon. I **(19)** _____ (find out) I **(20)** _____ (make) a terrible mistake as soon as I **(21)** _____ (see) the check-in counter. On the schedule board, I read "Arrivals and departures for Tuesday, September 3." Was that today? Of course not. I **(22)** _____ (come) to the airport a day too early!

# 8

## Listening 🔊

**5** 🎧 Play track 18. Listen to the two people talking at an airport. Complete the sentences with the correct choice.

**1.** Lou is the woman's _____.

    **a.** husband

    **b.** friend

    **c.** brother

**2.** Lou had gotten to the airport late because _____.

    **a.** he couldn't get a taxi

    **b.** there was a lot of traffic

    **c.** he'd had a late meeting

**3.** When Lou reached the gate, his plane was _____.

    **a.** at the gate

    **b.** almost on the runway

    **c.** in the air

**4.** Lou made his flight because he _____ .

    **a.** told a lie

    **b.** was getting married

    **c.** knew the pilot

**6** 🎧 Play track 18 again. What do you hear? Listen and circle *a* or *b*.

**1. a.** What happened?

   **b.** What had happened?

**2. a.** Lou was on a business trip.

   **b.** Lou had been on a business trip.

**3. a.** He got to the airport late.

   **b.** He had gotten to the airport late.

**4. a.** He was late for his real wedding.

   **b.** He had been late for his real wedding.

## Pronunciation 🔊

**7** 🎧 Play track 19. Notice the pronunciation of the contracted and weak forms of *had*. Listen and fill in the blanks. Use contractions where appropriate.

**1.** _____ _____ my book.

**2.** I realized _____ _____ _____ it in the café.

**3.** _____ already _____ out of the hotel.

**4.** He was late because _____ _____ stuck in traffic.

**5.** His plane _____ _____ left the gate.

**6.** But it _____ _____ off _____.

**8** 🎧 Play track 19 again. Listen and repeat.

## Reading

**9** Look at the photo and the title of the article. What do you think the article will be about?

_____

**10** Read the article. What happens to almost all of the unclaimed luggage?

**a.** It is destroyed.  **b.** It is auctioned off.  **c.** It is sold.

# Lost and Found? No, **LOST** and **SOLD!**

Before checking their bags at the airport, most people carefully **attach** ID tags to them with their name, address, and phone number. But no matter how much care is taken, sometimes things get lost.

Actually, in the U.S., only .005 percent of all checked bags get **permanently** lost. But this **adds up** to a significant number since we're talking about millions of people and pieces of luggage. If, after 90 days, the airline is unable to find the owner of a piece of luggage, then it is officially declared **"unclaimed."**

So what happens to these unclaimed bags and the things inside them? Most of them go to a store in Scottsboro, Alabama, called Unclaimed Baggage, to be resold. Thousands of items come into the store every day—over a million items a year!

The prices on items at Unclaimed Baggage are much cheaper than those in regular stores. You can often find great **deals,** especially because people **tend** to take their nicest things with them when they travel. You can even purchase items online!

But don't go to Unclaimed Baggage to look for something specific that you lost while traveling. By the time the luggage arrives at the store, the airlines have already made every effort to return the bag to its owner, and the items at the store are unmarked.

Here is just a partial list of **goods** you can **purchase**—many brand new!

- digital camcorders
- CD players
- binoculars
- computer accessories
- scarves
- designer coats
- sunglasses
- leather jackets

**11** Read the article again and answer these questions.

**1.** According to the article, how many bags are lost?

    **a.** 5 out of every 100    **b.** 5 out of every 1,000    **c.** 5 out of every 10,000

**2.** When is a piece of luggage considered "unclaimed"?

    **a.** when the airline has not found its owner after 90 days

    **b.** when no one has come for it within 90 days

    **c.** when it arrives at the baggage claim without any ID tags on it

**12** Find the word in bold that means

    **a.** forever _____    **b.** products _____    **c.** be likely to _____

45

# Self-Quiz for Units 5–8

## Vocabulary

### UNIT 5

**A**  Match each behavior on the left with an alternative that is more polite in the U.S.

**1.** point at someone ___C___

**2.** eat with your fingers _____

**3.** snap your fingers _____

**4.** have your elbows on the table _____

**5.** reach across the table _____

**6.** have your feet up on the chair _____

**a.** keep your hands under the table

**b.** keep your feet on the floor

**c.** describe the person you're talking about

**d.** ask a person to pass something

**e.** use a fork, knife, and spoon

**f.** say "Excuse me" to get someone's attention

### UNIT 6

**B**  Write the verbs *achieve, come up with, invent, overcome, pass,* or *solve* before the appropriate pair of nouns.

**1.** ___invent___ a machine / a device

**2.** _____ an idea / a solution

**3.** _____ an obstacle / a problem

**4.** _____ a problem / a puzzle

**5.** _____ an exam / a course

**6.** _____ a goal / an objective

### UNIT 7

**C**  Write *T* (true) or *F* (false) after each sentence.

**1.** If you get away with a crime, then the police catch you. ___F___

**2.** You usually tell people if you're going to eavesdrop on their conversations. _____

**3.** I ask you to keep an eye on something if I want you to watch it. _____

**4.** If you commit a crime, you do something illegal. _____

**5.** Private detectives try to spy on a person without that person knowing. _____

**6.** A person's movements are restricted if his or her movements are limited. _____

### UNIT 8

**D**  Complete each sentence with the words *baggage claim, check-in counter, flight attendant, gate, luggage,* or *security checkpoint.*

**1.** You pack all the things you'll take in your _luggage_.

**2.** You go to the _____ to get your boarding pass.

**3.** People at a _____ make sure you don't carry anything dangerous onto the airplane.

**4.** You wait at the _____ to get on the plane.

**5.** A _____ brings you food and drinks on the plane.

**6.** You get off the plane and go to the _____ to get your luggage.

# Grammar

## UNIT 5

**A** Use the words in parentheses to rewrite the sentences as questions.

1. I need to look at your calendar. **(can)** _Can I look at your calendar?_

2. I want to borrow your car. **(may)** _____

3. I need to use your phone. **(could)** _____

4. I'd like to sit here. **(would you mind)** _____

5. I want to order a drink. **(do you mind)** _____

6. I have to arrive a little late. **(is it OK if)** _____

## UNIT 6

**B** Complete the sentences with the present perfect or the present perfect continuous of the verbs in parentheses.

1. The team _has won_ several prizes this year. **(win)**

2. I _____ a lot of healthful foods recently, and I feel good. **(eat)**

3. Dylan _____ several articles about Mars. **(publish)**

4. Your assistant _____ all the files yet. **(not receive)**

5. She _____ English a lot at work, and she's really improving. **(speak)**

6. We _____ hard all morning, so let's take a break now. **(work)**

## UNIT 7

**C** Complete the sentences with *in order to*, *so that*, *in case*, or *for*.

1. We keep candles in our house _in case_ the lights go out.

2. Some people get dogs _____ they feel safer at home.

3. Stores use security cameras _____ reduce shoplifting.

4. I always carry a cell phone _____ I can contact my family.

5. Take your cell phone with you _____ I need to talk to you.

6. The bank has a camera _____ recording all transactions.

## UNIT 8

**D** Complete each sentence with two words or phrases from the box.

| | | | |
|---|---|---|---|
| checked | ~~didn't order~~ | didn't enjoy | ~~had already eaten~~ |
| had already heard | had left | had made | had seen |
| hadn't eaten | knew | read | were |

1. She _had already eaten_ , so she _didn't order_ anything at the restaurant.

2. When I _____ my email, Jeff _____ me a message.

3. He _____ the movie because he_____ it before.

4. By the time I _____ the paper, I _____ the news on the radio.

5. They _____ very hungry because they _____ anything since breakfast.

6. The student _____ he _____ a mistake as soon as he saw the professor's face.

# Sunshine and showers

## Vocabulary

**1**  Match the words with the pictures.

cloud cover __c__   clouds _____   fog _____   rain _____   shower _____

snow _____   sunshine _____   thunderstorm _____   tornado _____   wind _____

a.

f.

b.

g.

c.

h.

d.

i.

e.

j.

**2**  Complete the weather reports with the correct word from Exercise 1.

**1.** It's now dry here in the city, but there is a very thick ___cloud cover___. The _____ are getting darker and darker. In fact, the _____ is on its way, and it could be heavy at times. Floods are possible.

**2.** If you're driving to work this morning, be very careful. You probably won't be able to see the car in front of you because of the dense _____ that has covered the area. Don't expect this to last too long, though, because by 10 A.M., we should have lots of _____ and blue skies.

**3.** A member of Kennedy High's golf team was injured today when he was hit by lightning during a _____. Witnesses say the young man was standing under a tree when the incident occurred.

**4.** Skiers, celebrate! Lots of _____ is expected to fall tonight, making tomorrow a perfect day to hit the slopes. It will be a chilly day, but there won't be much _____ blowing that snow around, so enjoy!

# Grammar

**3** Change each direct statement to an indirect statement. Imagine that the speaker is a man.

> **1.** I'm tired of the heat.

> **5.** I listened to the weather forecast in the morning.

> **2.** I have plans with some friends for the weekend.

> **6.** I lost five umbrellas.

> **3.** It was raining a lot.

> **7.** I can't stand cold weather.

> **4.** We were indoors all day.

> **8.** I will move to a warmer place.

He said that . . .

**1.** _he was tired of the heat._

**2.** _____

**3.** _____

**4.** _____

**5.** _____

**6.** _____

**7.** _____

**8.** _____

**4** Two neighbors, Gina and Tom, are talking about the terrible hurricane that they recently survived. Rewrite their conversation in indirect speech. Make any necessary changes.

**Gina:** **(1)** Your house looks OK.

**Tom:** **(2)** We're very lucky that the roof didn't blow off.

**Gina:** **(3)** My family wasn't that lucky.

**Tom:** **(4)** I can see that.

**Gina:** **(5)** We'll stay at a hotel tonight.

**Tom:** **(6)** You can stay with us.

**Gina:** **(7)** That's very nice of you.

**Tom:** **(8)** We're all going to have to help one another.

**1.** Gina told Tom that _his house looked OK_____.

**2.** Tom said _____.

**3.** Gina said that _____.

**4.** Tom replied that _____.

**5.** Gina told Tom _____.

**6.** Tom said that _____.

**7.** Gina said that _____.

**8.** Tom told Gina _____.

## Listening

**5** 🎧 Play track 20. Listen for the details and complete the notes.

1. Hurricanes have two main components: The _____ of the hurricane and the wall of _____ around it.

2. The eye is a _____ area in the _____ of the _____.

3. A tornado is a column of _____ that _____ with _____ violence.

4. It's so hard to _____ when _____ are coming.

5. Tornados can rip houses out of their foundations and _____ them _____ in the _____.

**6** 🎧 Read the sentences. Then play track 20 again. Circle the words that correctly complete the sentences.

1. *Typhoon* is a word more commonly used in **Asia / North America**.

2. One thing that hurricanes and tornadoes have in common is **strong winds / heavy rain**.

3. The word the weather forecaster uses to describe both hurricanes and tornadoes is *tropical / violent*.

4. Most hurricanes, typhoons, and tornadoes probably occur in **warm / cold** weather.

## Pronunciation

**7** 🎧 Play track 67. Listen. Notice the pronunciation of the *th* sounds. Write the words in the correct column.

| /θ/ like *south* | /ð/ like *that* |
|---|---|
| there | |
| | |
| | |
| | |
| | |

**8** 🎧 Play track 68. Listen. Fill in the blanks.

1. What did _____ say about _____ _____?

2. _____ said _____ would be _____ clouds and _____.

**9** 🎧 Play track 68 again. Listen and repeat.

## Reading

**10** Think about the seasons of the year. During which one is there the least sunlight in the northern hemisphere of the Earth?

    **a.** summer      **b.** fall      **c.** winter      **d.** spring

**11** Read the article. Match the headings below with the correct paragraphs.

    **a.** What causes SAD? _3_      **b.** Who gets SAD? _____      **c.** What are the symptoms? _____

    **d.** How is SAD treated? _____      **e.** What is SAD? _____

# SAD on gloomy days?

Do you get sad in the winter? Seasonal affective **disorder** (SAD) is a type of depression that some people experience during the winter months. It starts as the days get shorter and colder, and it lasts until summer, when symptoms usually disappear. SAD is far more intense than common "winter blues" or "winter blahs," which many people complain of from time to time.

A **craving** for sugary or starchy foods, weight gain, a **tendency** to sleep more, decreased energy levels, **moodiness**, and even feelings of hopelessness are all possible symptoms of SAD. Patients report that their **fatigue** and moodiness tend to increase as the day wears on.

The disorder is caused mainly by lack of sunlight in winter. As seasons change, there is an impact on the body's "circadian rhythms"—the bodily functions that go through cycles every 24 hours.

People who live in regions far north or south of the equator are more likely to suffer from SAD. For example, SAD is far less common in Florida than in Canada. In fact, SAD patients report great improvement when visiting places with more sunlight in winter.

SAD is sometimes treated with special light boxes prescribed by doctors. (This is not the same as tanning beds, which have harmful ultraviolet rays.) Some doctors prescribe antidepressant medications for extreme SAD cases. Of course, the **ultimate** remedy is to move to a place with a sunny climate year round!

**12** Read the article again. Complete the phrases on the left with the information on the right to make true statements. You will not need all the choices on the right.

    **1.** Seasonal affective disorder is _____      **a.** cold weather.

    **2.** SAD is caused by _____      **b.** sadness and weight gain.

    **3.** The symptoms of SAD include _____      **c.** a contagious disease.

    **4.** SAD doesn't usually cause _____      **d.** lack of sunlight.

    **e.** fever and loss of appetite.

    **f.** a feeling of depression.

**13** Find the word in bold that means

    **a.** definite _____      **b.** a desire _____      **c.** extreme tiredness _____

# Tomorrow's world

## Vocabulary

**1** Look at the word pairs in the box. Are they synonyms (S) or antonyms (A)? Label them *S* or *A*.

| | |
|---|---|
| improve / worsen __A__ | strengthen / weaken _____ |
| fall / drop _____ | deteriorate / worsen _____ |
| increase / decrease _____ | decline / decrease _____ |
| increase / climb _____ | get better / get worse _____ |
| go up / climb _____ | rise / decline _____ |

**2** Choose all the words or phrases from Exercise 1 that correctly complete each sentence. Use the appropriate forms.

1. The temperature is _dropping_ / _falling_ / _decreasing_ fast. It's really cold out, and I think it's going to snow any minute.

2. Poor Mr. Jones's condition has _____ / _____ / _____ / _____ / _____ overnight. His doctor doesn't know when he'll be able to leave the hospital.

3. The quality of life in this city seems to _____ / _____ every year. We're very lucky to live here.

4. The new factory has hired many workers from the town, and the unemployment rate has _____ / _____ / _____ / _____ to a new low.

5. The curtain _____ / _____ , and the singer walked out on the stage.

6. What causes the price of gasoline to change so frequently? It has _____ / _____ / _____ / _____ by 20 percent since last month, and many people can't afford to drive their cars.

# Grammar

**3** Complete the sentences with the simple future or the future perfect of the verbs in parentheses. More than one answer is possible in some cases.

**Lisa:** Over the next few minutes, Joshua Frye and I will **(1)** _discuss_ (discuss) some predictions about the future. I'm sure most of our listeners will **(2)** _____ (recognize) Josh from last Saturday's program. Welcome back, Josh.

**Josh:** Thanks, Lisa. Nice to be here.

**Lisa:** Our audience will **(3)** _____ (be) happy to know that by the end of today's segment, they'll **(4)** _____ (hear) some good news about the future—for a change.

**Josh:** That's right. One question that I hear a lot is whether the world's oil supply will **(5)** _____ (run out) by the start of the next century.

**Lisa:** And what's your opinion on that?

**Josh:** I believe—as do many experts—that we will **(6)** _____ (start) using less and less oil very soon. I have no doubt that before the oil supply is in danger, scientists will already **(7)** _____ (make) great advances in alternative energy sources such as solar and wind energy. In fact, by the end of this century, we'll **(8)** _____ (replace) oil entirely.

**Lisa:** That does sound like good news. What about the world's population? How many of us will there **(9)** _____ (be) in the twenty-second century?

**Josh:** That's a tough question. I can tell you that the population will **(10)** _____ (reach) at least 7.8 billion in the next 25 years. And we are hopeful that, to quote a twentieth-century philosopher, someday soon we will **(11)** _____ (succeed) at creating a "world that works for everyone."

**Lisa:** Do you believe it will **(12)** _____ (be) possible to eliminate hunger and poverty in all the world within our lifetime?

**Josh:** Yes, I do.

**4** Correct the mistakes in the sentences. Be careful: One sentence is correct.

1. By the time you read this, I ~~will go~~ _will have gone_ home.

2. Will you graduate by this time next year?

3. On January 1, we will be knowing each other for six months.

4. Most people agree that the future will bring many changes.

5. Will he receive my letter yet?

6. By this time next year, I will be here for three years.

53

*10*

## Listening 🔊

**5** 🎧 **Play track 22. Circle the words or phrases that correctly complete the sentences.**

1. Dr. Pierce (has)/ hasn't been on "Changing Times" before.

2. "A Frankenstein future" would be caused by people using technology for **good / bad** purposes.

3. The tiny computer that will monitor people's body functions will be available by the year **2099 / 2999**.

4. The interviewer **thinks / doesn't think** the device designed to monitor body functions would be a good use of technology.

5. Dr. Pierce **is / isn't** sure there will be computers that will connect with people's brains.

6. Dr. Pierce is worried that computers could replace **schools / students**.

**6** 🎧 **Play track 22 again. Answer the questions. Write complete sentences.**

1. The interviewer and Dr. Pierce talk about a tiny computer that will monitor body functions. How will the computer get into the body?

   *People will swallow the computers.*

2. How will the device that monitors body functions affect our health care?

   _____

3. What won't students learn if they can simply download information into their brains?

   _____

4. What will happen to intelligent thought if we're able to download information into our brain?

   _____

## Pronunciation 🔊

**7** 🎧 **Play track 23. Notice the pronunciation of the contracted and weak forms of *will* and the way *will* is linked to the weak form of *have*. Listen and fill in the blanks. Write contractions where appropriate.**

1. _____ be able to swallow tiny computers.

2. _____ record what's going on.

3. Communication _____ _____ easier.

4. Scientists _____ _____ perfected the brainlink computer.

5. _____ _____ learned to communicate by brainwaves.

6. _____ _____ found ways to read people's thoughts.

**8** 🎧 **Play track 23 again. Listen and repeat.**

## Reading

**9** Look at the pictures. Which one illustrates "parallel parking"?

a.

b.

**10** Read the article. What are two things the Prius can't do while parking itself?

_____

_____

# THE CAR OF THE FUTURE?

The part of the driving test that most student drivers dread is when they have to parallel park their car. It is tricky, after all, to drive in reverse while you aim your car so it glides smoothly into the space between two other parked cars, without touching the curb. But the time may soon come when drivers will never have to park their own cars again. The Japanese car manufacturer Toyota recently launched a model of its hybrid car Prius that can park itself.

The Prius is already one of the most futuristic–and environmentally friendly–cars available on the market. For its new self-parking option, the Prius uses a built-in computer and camera to back the car into a parking spot while avoiding white parking lines and other cars. Theoretically, the human driver never has to touch the steering wheel.

But the Prius' self-parking system has some limitations: it won't stop for moving objects, so you still have to hit the brakes yourself, and it will only work when you can continuously back up into a space, rather than inching backwards and forwards to squeeze your way in. That makes it ineffective in the trickiest parallel-parking situations, just when it would be the most useful.

Although it will be some time before a truly self-driving vehicle is available to consumers, industry observers are excited about the Prius's self-parking option, seeing it as an important step towards self-driving cars.

**11** Read the article again. Write _T_ (true) or _F_ (false) after each statement.

1. The self-parking car controls the steering wheel by itself. _____

2. The Prius would stop automatically if a child ran behind it while it is parking. _____

3. The self-parking car is a first step towards self-driving cars. _____

**12** Find the word in the article that means

a. introduced a new product to the public (paragraph 1) _____

b. restrictions on what something is able to do (paragraph 3) _____

# How did it go?

## Vocabulary

**1** Complete the crossword puzzle.

**Across**

**3** A better position in the company that you get for doing a good job, usually after a few years

**5** Written reports about you and your work from past employers

**6** Things you're not good at

**9** Work experience, certificates, and degrees are all types of these

**Down**

**1** Jobs you've done in the past

**2** A word that means "opportunities or possibilities for getting a better job"

**4** A situation where people ask you questions to find out if you should get the job

**7** Things you're good at

**8** Plans and aims for your future

1. e
   x
3. p
   e
   r
   i
   e
   n
   c
   e

**2** Complete the business letter with words from Exercise 1.

Dear Mr. Mendoza:

I'm writing to follow up on the **(1)** _interview_ that I had at your company yesterday. It was a pleasure meeting you, and I hope that you will find my **(2)** _____ suited to the position of assistant manager. I believe my business degree and the management **(3)** _____ that I acquired at my last two jobs make me a worthy candidate for the job.

I was very honest about my **(4)** _____ and **(5)** _____: as with most people, there are some things I do well and others that are not always easy for me. My last two employers are willing to provide **(6)** _____, so please feel free to let me know if you'd like to see them.

# Grammar

**3** Todd is a human resources officer at a bank. He's telling his supervisor about some of the questions he asked a job applicant during an interview today. Change the direct questions to indirect questions. Make any necessary changes.

1. What job are you applying for?

   I asked him ___what job he was applying for___.

2. How did you find out about the job?

   I wanted to know _____.

3. Did you graduate from college?

   I asked him _____.

4. How long have you been working in your present position?

   I was curious about _____.

5. How much work experience have you had?

   I needed to know _____.

6. Is there someone we can contact for references?

   I asked _____.

7. Can I call your current boss?

   I wanted him to tell me _____.

8. When will you be able to start?

   I wanted to know _____.

**4** After Sophia's interview for a new job, she emailed her friend to tell her about it. Find and correct the six mistakes with indirect or direct questions. The first mistake has been corrected for you.

I'm writing to tell you about my interview. I wasn't nervous at all even

though there were three people there. First they asked me if ~~am I~~ `I was` good with

computers and what  software have I used. They also wanted to know if can I

drive. So that was OK. Then the woman asked me you have any questions.

After that, they wanted to know my strengths. I said I was very good with

people. They asked if I will can start next month. Finally, one of the men

wanted to know when can I give them my decision. So that means that I got

the job. I'm so happy! :>)

How about you? Did you have a good time with that guy you met? Send me ALL

the details.

## Listening

**5** Play track 24. Listen to Carol tell her friend about the job interview she had earlier in the day. Circle the answer that correctly completes the sentences.

1. The interviewer was interested in **why** / **when** she'd left her other jobs.

2. Carol thought the interview went badly because she **didn't talk enough / talked too much**.

3. Carol's friend thought **"What are your strengths?"** / **"What are your weaknesses?"** was a difficult question to answer.

4. Carol told the interviewer being a perfectionist was one of her **strengths / weaknesses**.

5. Carol's friend **liked / didn't like** her answer to the interviewer's question about her weaknesses.

**6** Play track 24 again. Listen and fill in the missing verbs.

1. She _____ me to _____ her what experience I _____.

2. She _____ me about all my previous jobs and why I _____ _____ them and what kind of responsibilities I _____ _____.

3. She _____ to _____ what my strengths and weaknesses _____.

## Pronunciation

**7** Play track 25. Notice the groups of consonant sounds in some of the words in the sentences. Listen and repeat the isolated words. Then listen to the sentences and fill in the blanks.

1. She _____ about my _____ _____.

2. She _____ me what my _____ were.

3. I _____ her I _____ well under _____.

4. I _____ her about the _____ for _____.

5. She _____ me how long I _____ to _____.

6. She _____ me when I could _____.

**8** Play track 25 again. Listen and repeat.

# Reading

**9** Look at the title of the article and the jobs in the headings. Which job do you think . . .

can be done from home? _____

is not usually done in the same location every day? _____

requires advanced education? _____

**10** Read the article. Match the jobs in the article with the quotes.

a. "It hurts if we lose one, but I always try to learn from it so we can save the next one." _____

b. "Some of them are just lonely or sad. I try to make them feel better." _____

c. "I found out that some of them were rude!" _____

# ODD JOBS

## Have you ever thought about getting an unconventional job? Consider these occupations:

### Mystery shopper

Imagine being paid to go shopping, eat in a restaurant, or stay at a hotel. That's what mystery shoppers do. They are ordinary people hired to **pose** as shoppers and customers at stores or other places of business in order to evaluate products and services **anonymously**. They look for such things as: How helpful and friendly was the staff? Was the service prompt? How clean was the site? Employers use this **feedback** to monitor employees and improve their businesses.

### Zoo doctor

On any given day, a zoo veterinarian performs such tasks as weighing animals, checking on newborns, and tending to minor injuries. Preventive medicine and grooming are important. For example, when examining a large bear, the vet might take blood **samples**, clean and polish the bear's teeth, clip his claws, and weigh him, usually with several people moving the sedated animal onto the scale. Zoos have many different **species**, from fish to gorillas to tigers. Zoo vets can't specialize and know how to treat every animal, but there is a network of zoo vets who consult each other.

### Telephone psychic

Is it entertainment, spiritual **counseling**, or a **rip-off**? Thousands of people call psychic hotlines for advice about love, relationships, or money, trusting that the person on the other end has special powers. The "psychics," who may be unemployed actors, sometimes believe they really have extrasensory gifts, but most of the time they read a script while claiming to see the future. The most common question from callers is: "Is this stuff for real?"

**11** Read the article again. Write *T* (true) or *F* (false). The author believes that . . .

1. businesses can be helped by mystery shoppers. _____

2. zoo vets must have extensive knowledge about every zoo animal. _____

3. telephone psychics are not always honest. _____

**12** Find the word in bold that means

a. pretend to be _____

b. something that makes you feel cheated _____

c. groups of animals that can breed with each other _____

# Coincidences

## Vocabulary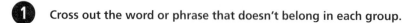

**1** Cross out the word or phrase that doesn't belong in each group.

1. every time          each time          ~~at the same time~~          whenever

2. previously          afterwards          earlier          before

3. at the same moment          subsequently          at the same time          simultaneously

4. simultaneously          afterwards          later          subsequently

**2** Circle the correct choice to complete each sentence.

1. I'm in the middle of something, and I really need to finish it by 3:00. Can I call you back (**later**) / **afterwards**?

2. Both lectures are being held **at the same moment / simultaneously**. I can't decide which one to go to.

3. **At the same time / Every time** it rains, our roof leaks. I think it's time to get it fixed.

4. **Whenever / At the same time** Kristy and John discuss politics, they end up getting into an argument. Why don't they just avoid the topic altogether?

5. Governor Smith lost the election and **simultaneously / later** announced he was retiring from public life.

6. When Stephen King's latest book was published, many people already knew about it because he had **previously / subsequently** discussed it on a TV talk show.

7. Ms. Santos and Mr. Adams are both going to give the oral exam this term so that two students can be tested **at the same time / previously**. That way, students won't have to wait so long.

8. When the much-anticipated sequel finally opened in theaters across the country, many fans had **at the same time / previously** bought their tickets online.

9. During the snowstorm, a truck driver lost control of his vehicle and caused a ten-car accident. Many victims were taken to the hospital, but they were **simultaneously / later** released.

# Grammar

**3** Read the story. Complete the sentences with the correct past tense form of the verbs.

## Shock in the Desert

I **(1)** _had lived_ (live) in Arizona for about six months when I **(2)** _____ (decide) that I needed a vacation. Things were pretty crazy at the office, and what I **(3)** _____ (want) was a little peace and quiet. So I **(4)** _____ (decide) to go away for a few days. Several weeks earlier, someone **(5)** _____ (tell) me about a lovely desert resort outside the city. I **(6)** _____ (call) and **(7)** _____ (reserve) a room for four nights.

Friday evening, after work, I **(8)** _____ (go) home and **(9)** _____ (pick up) my suitcase, which I **(10)** _____ (pack) the night before. I **(11)** _____ (look forward to) a change. I **(12)** _____ (get) to the resort in a little over an hour. I **(13)** _____ (check in) and **(14)** _____ (go) to my room. The sun **(15)** _____ (set) in the west, and the view from my window was breathtaking! I **(16)** _____ (know) at that moment that I **(17)** _____ (make) the right decision.

I **(18)** _____ (be) at the resort for two days when I **(19)** _____ (get) the shock of my life. It was late afternoon, and I **(20)** _____ (read) when suddenly I saw something out of the corner of my eye. I **(21)** _____ (turn) to look and **(22)** _____ (see) this huge scorpion.

At first, I just **(23)** _____ (freeze). Then I **(24)** _____ (jump) out of the chair. After I **(25)** _____ (calm down), I **(26)** _____ (take off) my shoe. While the scorpion **(27)** _____ (crawl) up the wall, I **(28)** _____ (aim) and **(29)** _____ (hit) it with my shoe. It was only a lot later that I realized I **(30)** _____ (never be) so scared in my whole life!

The strangest thing was when I **(31)** _____ (get back) to the city Tuesday night, I **(32)** _____ (discover) that my assistant **(33)** _____ (spend) two days in the hospital. Early Monday morning, she **(34)** _____ (find) a scorpion in my office, and it **(35)** _____ (sting) her!

## Listening

**4** 🎧 **Play track 26. Listen to the man's story. Complete the sentences with the correct choice.**

1. The man's first reaction when he saw the smoke on the road was to feel _____.

   **a.** annoyed          **b.** frightened

2. When the man first got out of his car, he _____.

   **a.** knew he had to help    **b.** didn't know what to do

3. The young woman trapped in the car was the _____.

   **a.** driver          **b.** passenger

4. When the young woman was dragged to safety, the man knew she was alive because she _____.

   **a.** was breathing      **b.** spoke to him

5. The man realized who the young woman was when _____.

   **a.** he saw her face      **b.** she spoke to him

**5** 🎧 **Play track 26 again. Circle the expression you hear.**

1. I **stayed / had stayed** late at the office.

2. A car **slammed / had slammed** into a tree.

3. Evidently, she **was trying / had been trying** to get help.

4. Together, he and I **managed / had managed** to drag the other person out.

5. After we **pulled / had pulled** her to safety, it was still too dark to see her face.

## Pronunciation

**6** 🎧 **Play track 28. Notice the stress on the important words. Underline the words that carry the main stress.**

Irene Jones and Stella Frank, both from Texas, grew up on the same street and became best friends. Stella was Irene's bridesmaid at her wedding. Then Irene moved away, and they lost touch. Fifty-three years later, they bumped into each other while they were waiting in line at a gas station in Boulder, Colorado.

**7** 🎧 **Play track 28 again. Listen and repeat.**

## Reading

**8** What is a curse?

    **a.** a strange and unbelievable story      **c.** a bad wish for someone

    **b.** a class in a particular subject      **d.** a kind of wrapping or cover

**9** Read the article. What did Carter and Lord Carnarvon find inside the tomb? Check (✓) all the correct answers.

    _____ **a.** jewels and coins          _____ **c.** writings on stone

    _____ **b.** food and beverages      _____ **d.** tools and pottery

# An Ancient Mummy's Curse, or Coincidence?

In 1922, British Egyptologists Howard Carter and Lord Carnarvon **excavated** the tomb of the ancient Egyptian King Tutankhamen. With a team of twenty-five others, Carter and Carnarvon entered the tomb and found it full of treasures and many other artifacts. They also found a tablet with hieroglyphs. When they translated the writings, they discovered that it warned of a curse that would fall on anyone who **dared** to enter the tomb and remove the king's possessions.

Seven weeks later, Lord Carnarvon became ill from an infected insect bite on his cheek and died. When the mummy was unwrapped in 1925, scientists **observed** a wound on the mummy's left cheek in the same spot as the fatal bite on Carnarvon's face.

Newspapers from around the world said that Carnarvon's death was the result of the "mummy's curse." Scientists, on the other hand, **speculated** that Carnarvon was exposed to some ancient infection that **got into** his body through the wound caused by the bite.

To this day, the mystery of the 3,000-year-old curse remains. Was the death of a leading archaeologist the result of a curse, or were the archaeologist's death and a wound on a mummy's cheek merely a coincidence?

**10** Read the article again. Complete the sentences with the correct information.

    **1.** The writings in the tomb warned against _____.

    **2.** Many journalists wrote that Carnarvon's death was _____.

    **3.** Scientists believed that the real cause of Lord Carnarvon's death was _____.

**11** Find the word in bold that means

    **a.** dug up _____      **a.** hypothesized _____      **c.** risked _____

# Self-Quiz for Units 9–12

## Vocabulary

### UNIT 9

**A** Match each word with a piece of advice.

1. sunshine __e__
2. cloud cover _____
3. fog _____
4. tornado _____
5. thunderstorm _____
6. shower _____

a. Avoid driving if you can.
b. You should carry an umbrella.
c. Stay in an underground shelter if you can.
d. You should stay away from trees.
e. Use sunscreen if you have sensitive skin.
f. It probably won't rain, but cancel your beach plans.

### UNIT 10

**B** Circle the word that means the opposite of each word in bold.

1. The weather conditions have **deteriorated**.   worsened   (gotten better)
2. His health **improved**.   strengthened   deteriorated
3. Unemployment rates **fell**.   climbed   declined
4. Sales **increased**.   went up   dropped
5. Traffic has **gotten better**.   worsened   improved
6. The crime rate is **decreasing**.   falling   climbing

### UNIT 11

**C** Circle the appropriate word to complete each sentence.

1. A (long-term goal) / reference is something that you want to do in the future.
2. A move to a more important job or position in a company is a **prospect / promotion**.
3. A **qualification / reference** is something you say or write about the work of another person.
4. A certain quality or ability that gives someone an advantage is a **strength / long-term goal**.
5. Something that is possible or is likely to happen in the future is a **qualification / prospect**.
6. **Experience / qualifications** are skills or personal qualities that make you able to do a particular job.

### UNIT 12

**D** Complete each sentence with *afterwards, at the same time, earlier, every time, previously, simultaneously, subsequently,* or *whenever*. Some sentences have more than one possible answer.

1. The speaker first answered the questions that people had __previously__ emailed.
2. We have a client meeting until 12:30, but _____ I'm free to go to lunch.
3. At first no one said anything, then everyone started to talk _____.
4. I think of you _____ I use the coffee mug you gave me.
5. _____ you have a minute, Luis needs your help.
6. The company lowered its prices, and _____ sales increased.

# Grammar

## UNIT 9

 Rewrite the sentences in indirect speech. Make any necessary changes.

1. Laura told her husband, "We need to get milk on the way home."
   *Laura told her husband that they needed to get milk on the way home.*
2. The reporter said, "The storm will get worse before it gets better."

3. Ursula said, "I really want to go with you, but I can't."

4. Mr. Greer told his daughter, "I'll read you a story after you get in bed."

5. James said, "I saw the movie earlier this week."

6. The spokesperson told the press, "The governor made a decision in the morning."

## UNIT 10

 Complete each sentence with the future or future perfect form of the verbs in parentheses.

1. Do you think that people <u>will have traveled</u> to Mars by the year 2020? **(travel)**

2. Some experts believe that eventually the population _____ to decrease. **(begin)**

3. Hopefully scientists _____ a cure for cancer soon. **(discover)**

4. Within 50 years, people _____ hybrid cars. **(get used to)**

5. Computers _____ much smaller by the time our children have them. **(become)**

6. Protection of the environment_____ important in the future. **(remain)**

## UNIT 11

 Complete each sentence to make an indirect question. Use the cues in parentheses.

1. The tourist asked, "Where is the opera house?" **(the tourist asked)**
   *The tourist asked where the opera house was.*
2. The customer asked, "What time does the store open?" **(The customer wanted to know)**

3. The interviewer asked me, "Do you have experience in sales?" **(He wanted me to tell him if)**

4. Our friends asked, "Did you enjoy yourselves?" **(They wanted to know whether)**

5. A woman asked me, "How much did you pay for the jacket?" **(She wanted me to tell her)**

6. Ken asked Shari, "Will you be able to make it to the party?" **(He asked her whether)**

## UNIT 12

D Complete each sentence with the simple past, the past continuous, the past perfect, or the past perfect continuous of the verbs in parentheses.

Ellen and Edward grew up on the same street but lost contact when Ellen moved away with her family. One day, Ellen had a flat tire on her way to work. Edward was driving by and stopped to help. Edward and Ellen **(1)** *didn't recognize* **(not recognize)** each other at first because they **(2)** _____ **(not see)** each other for so long. While they **(3)** _____ **(talk)**, they **(4)** _____ **(realized)** that they **(5)** _____ **(live)** on the same street when they were children. Before they knew it, they realized they **(6)** _____ **(talk)** for one hour and the tire was still flat!

# Going it alone

## Vocabulary

**1** Cross out the word or phrase that does not belong in each group.

| | | | |
|---|---|---|---|
| **1.** fearful | ~~jumpy~~ | terrified | petrified |
| **2.** cut off | solitary | isolated | tense |
| **3.** scared | jittery | jumpy | nervous |
| **4.** afraid | lonely | scared | fearful |
| **5.** lonesome | solitary | cut off | jittery |

**2** Complete the conversations with words from Exercise 1. More than one word is correct for some of the sentences. Try to use as many of the words as possible.

**1. A:** Why are you buying a house in the country? After living in the city for so many years, aren't you afraid you'll feel _____ being so far from civilization?

   **B:** Not at all. I'm very happy being by myself. And if I get _____, I can always call you.

**2. A:** Weren't you _____ when you lost control of the car?

   **B:** I was _____! It was the worst experience of my life.

**3. A:** You seem really _____. Is everything OK?

   **B:** No! It's work. We're all _____. The boss sent an email saying that the company would be downsizing in the new year.

**4. A:** Is Alison waiting for an important call? She seems _____, and she races to the phone each time it rings.

   **B:** Oh, you know Alison. She met a guy last week, and she's waiting to hear from him. She's _____ that he won't leave a message on voicemail.

# Grammar

**3** Complete the conversations with the correct form of the verbs. Use the present unreal conditional. Use contractions when possible.

1. **Ari:** How <u>would you feel</u> **(you/feel)** if you _____ **(get)** stuck in an elevator?

   **Dave:** If the doors _____ **(not open)**, I _____ **(not panic)**.

   I _____ **(try)** to stay calm. If I _____ **(have)** a cell phone with me,

   I _____ **(call)** for help. What _____ **(you/do)**?

   **Ari:** Oh, I really hate small spaces. I _____ **(not be)**

   calm at all. If I really _____ **(be)** stuck, I think

   I _____ **(scream)**.

2. **Pat:** You know, Bob, you _____ **(feel)** so much better if

   you _____ **(give up)** coffee and soda.

   **Bob:** So what _____ **(I/drink)** if I _____ **(stop)**

   drinking coffee and soda?

   **Pat:** That's a silly question. If you _____ **(know)** anything

   about staying healthy, you _____ **(know)** that we

   should drink at least eight glasses of water a day.

   **Bob:** Eight? If I _____ **(drink)** that much water, _____ **(drown)**!

**4** Write sentences using the present unreal conditional. Begin with the word in parentheses and make any necessary changes.

1. I don't have his email address. I want to write to him. **(If)**

   <u>If I had his email address, I'd write to him.</u>

2. He doesn't have time. He wants to finish the report today. **(If)**

   _____

3. We want to buy a horse. We don't have enough money. **(We)**

   _____

4. She doesn't study very hard. She always fails her exams. **(If)**

   _____

5. I'm not very rich. I don't know the winning lottery numbers. **(I)**

   _____

6. I want to do things differently. I can't live my life over again. **(I)**

   _____

# 13

## Listening

**5** 🎧 Play track 29. Listen to the radio show discussing Ellen MacArthur's life and correct the information. Read the sentences once before you listen.

*around the world*

1. The Jules Verne Challenge involves sailing nonstop ~~across the Atlantic.~~

2. Ellen MacArthur didn't think she and her crew could win the Jules Verne Challenge.

3. In the Jules Verne Challenge, there are strict limitations on the kind of boat and the number of crew members that competitors are allowed.

4. Ellen MacArthur is most afraid of strong competition.

5. Ellen bought her own boat by saving her babysitting money.

6. There were a total of four people on Ellen's boat for the Jules Verne Challenge.

**6** 🎧 Play track 29 again. Complete the sentences with the words you hear.

1. Always _____, Ellen said, "We _____ we can win it."

2. According to MacArthur, her biggest _____ is _____.

3. She decided that she _____ _____ again be _____ in a race.

4. Of course, there will be very _____ days.

5. That's what makes the _____ richer.

## Pronunciation

**7** 🎧 Play track 30. Listen. Notice the weak and contracted forms of *would* and the weak pronunciation of *could*. Fill in the blanks. Write contractions where appropriate.

1. If it weren't so cold, _____ go swimming.

2. I _____ do it if I were scared of being alone.

3. If you needed more sleep, you _____ never finish the race.

**8** 🎧 Play track 30 again. Listen and repeat.

## Reading

**9** Look at the picture of Charles Lindbergh. What do you think he was?

a. an airplane pilot _____

b. an astronaut _____

c. a race car driver _____

d. a ship's captain _____

**10** Read the article. Write *T* (true) or *F* (false) after each statement.

1. The first person to fly across the Atlantic was Charles Lindbergh. __F__
2. Lindbergh made the transatlantic trip by himself. _____
3. Transatlantic flight was not considered dangerous in the 1920s. _____
4. Lindbergh was tired before and during the flight. _____

# Charles Lindbergh, *"the lone eagle"*

In 1927 Charles Lindbergh was a 25-year-old airmail pilot with great aviation ideas. Though other pilots had flown across the Atlantic Ocean before, Lindbergh became the first to make the flight nonstop. And he did it alone.

A businessman had offered $25,000 (a fortune at the time) to the first aviator to fly between New York and Paris nonstop. Others had been killed or injured trying, but Lindbergh was **unafraid**. He believed that designing the right kind of airplane was key and convinced a group of St. Louis businessmen to help him build a single-engine airplane to make the trip. He called his plane "the Spirit of St. Louis." The newspapers called Lindbergh "the flying fool."

On May 20, 1927, a sleep-deprived Lindbergh packed five sandwiches, a bottle of water, and a compass before taking off from New York. The plane was so heavy with fuel that getting off the ground was a challenge, but he **managed** to become **airborne**. Because the plane had only one engine, any sort of trouble over the ocean could be fatal. Lindbergh understood that he might be facing death over the dark waters.

Fighting **drowsiness** and relying only on his compass to guide him, Lindbergh landed outside Paris 33½ hours later. He was **greeted** by an overjoyed crowd of over 100,000 French people and had to be "rescued" from the **throng**. On his return to New York, four million people attended a parade in his honor. No longer "the flying fool," he was **dubbed** "the lone eagle."

**11** Read the article again and complete the sentences.

Charles Lindbergh flew from _____ to _____ in _____ hours. It was the first

nonstop flight across the _____ .

**12** Find the word in bold that means

a. crowd _____

b. called _____

c. in the air _____

d. sleepiness _____

# UNIT 14

# Commuter blues

## Vocabulary

**1** Circle the correct word to complete the sentences.

1. What does Jason like to do in his (leisure)/ leave / leisurely time?

2. Will your doctor's appointment **spend / take / get** a long time?

3. **After / On / By** the time Sam's boss receives his letter of resignation, Sam will have accepted a new position in another company.

4. Nobuo never gets to class **in / on / at** time. He's always late.

5. Some people believe that watching TV is a **loss / waste / trash** of time. Not me!

6. Many companies these days give their employees time **off / out / of** when they have a personal emergency, such as a death in the family.

7. Susan is so self-confident that she believes it's only a matter **in / on / of** time until she becomes a star.

8. Many people lead such busy lives that they can't **spend / have / take** time doing the things they really enjoy.

9. With all this traffic, how will we get downtown **in / on / at** time to see the parade?

**2** Complete the sentences using the expressions with *time* from Exercise 1.

1. Ms. Lee is washing her windows today, but it's supposed to rain later. It's really a
   ___waste of time___ since they'll just get dirty again!

2. The Dawsons are never, ever late. They always arrive _____.

3. If we don't leave right now, we'll never make it _____ to see the beginning of the movie. It starts at 9:00, and it's already after 8:00.

4. You've been working too hard. Do you plan to take some _____ this year? I'm sure your company won't mind if you take a short vacation.

5. Kathy loves being with her grandparents. She likes to _____ with them every Sunday.

6. Medical school _____. Most doctors in the U.S. study for at least ten years before they can practice medicine.

7. We'd love to have more _____, but it seems all we do is work. It would be really nice to go out dancing once in a while.

8. Matt works long hours. _____ he gets home at night, his children are already in bed.

9. Everyone knows Tatiana and Phil will get together eventually. It's just _____.

# Grammar

**3** Complete the sentences with *although*, *despite (not)*, *however*, or *in spite of*. More than one answer is possible in some cases.

1. He felt sick. __However__ , he had to go to work.

2. He went to work, _____ feeling sick.

3. He went to work, _____ feeling well.

4. _____ it rained almost every day, we had a great time on our vacation.

5. _____ the terrible weather, we had a lot of fun.

6. We couldn't go to the beach much. _____ , we found other things to do.

7. He failed the exam, _____ all the studying he did.

8. He did poorly on the exam. _____ , he still passed the course.

9. The professor gave him a B for the term _____ his grade on the exam.

**4** Use the words in parentheses to combine the sentences to say what some students are doing wrong. Make all necessary changes.

1. School begins at 8:00. Yoko often arrives at 8:10. **(although)**

   _Although school begins at 8:00, Yoko often arrives at 8:10._

2. Tom lives right around the corner from the school. He's always late. **(in spite of)**

   _____

3. Lunch break is forty-five minutes. Stephanie always takes an hour. **(however)**

   _____

4. There is a strict cell phone policy. Ann is always calling her friends. **(in spite of)**

   _____

5. Students aren't allowed to eat in the gym. Sam often has lunch there. **(despite not)**

   _____

6. Students aren't supposed to wear hats. Rita sometimes wears hers. **(although)**

   _____

7. Pablo is getting very low scores on his tests. He's never at the library. **(despite)**

   _____

## Listening

**5** 🎧 Play track 31. Listen to two people talk about traveling to school and work. Write *T* (true) or *F* (false) next to each statement. Then correct the false statements. There may be more than one way to correct some sentences.

**1. a.** She lives very far from school. __F__

 **b.** Her first class probably starts at around the same time a lot of people start work. _____

 **c.** She probably goes to a small school. _____

 **d.** It takes her more than an hour to get to school. _____

**2. a.** Before he moved to the city, he lived in an awful place. _____

 **b.** Because of the noise and crowding, he wants to move out of the city. _____

 **c.** When it rains, he takes the bus to work. _____

 **d.** He's never too tired to walk home at the end of the day. _____

**6** 🎧 Play track 31 again. Complete the sentences with the words you hear.

**1.** It's amazing. _____ living only ten miles from school, I have a pretty long commute.

**2.** I used to live outside of town, and _____ it was a nice place, the commute was torture!

**3.** I'll never do it again. _____ the noise and crowding, I'm glad I live in the city.

## Pronunciation

**7** 🎧 Play track 32. Notice the pause in each sentence for the comma. Add a comma to each sentence.

**1.** You arrive at work tired. However, it could be a lot worse.

**2.** Although he knows the commuting time to the minute he leaves nothing to chance.

**3.** I usually get home relaxed despite the stress caused by a long day of hard work.

**4.** Despite living only ten miles from school I have a pretty long commute.

**5.** Despite not enjoying the trip he doesn't complain about it.

**6.** In spite of the noise and crowding I'm glad I live in the city.

**7.** In spite of staying with the same company all his life he still only gets ten days off a year.

**8** 🎧 Play track 32 again. Listen and repeat.

## Reading

**9** How do most people in cities in your country commute?

   **a.** by train   **b.** by car   **c.** by bicycle   **d.** other _____

**10** Read the article. Match each heading below with the appropriate list of reasons for biking.

**a.** Riding a bike helps you to feel good.

**b.** Riding a bike saves you money.

**c.** Riding a bike to work helps fight pollution.

**d.** Riding a bike saves you time.

### A Different Kind of Commute

In many places around the world, commuting doesn't mean driving a car; it means riding a bike. In some countries, the government not only **favors** biking, but it also makes it easy for cyclists. For example, in Münster, Germany, cyclists enjoy an extensive network of cycling routes, special traffic lights, and lots of space for bicycle parking.

In the U.S., biking to work or school isn't widespread. The League of American Cyclists, a group that **advocates** for commuting by bike, offers many reasons for people to leave their cars behind and hop on their bicycles.

**1.**
- Cars produce exhaust fumes that pollute the air, ground, and water.
- Gasoline engines create carbon dioxide ($CO_2$), which **damages** the Earth's ozone layer and **contributes** to global warming.

**2.**
- Biking to work lets you get a workout every day.
- You'll avoid the stress caused by sitting in traffic jams.
- You'll get to work refreshed and energetic.
- After work, you can use your commute home to ride off stress.
- You'll feel a sense of accomplishment from riding.

**3.**
- You can often ride past traffic by riding in bicycle lanes or by taking the back roads.
- You won't need to waste time looking for parking.

**4.**
- You won't spend as much on car maintenance and gas.
- You'll save money on parking (and tickets!).
- You won't have to join a gym to work out.

**11** Read the article again. Match the general reason for commuting by bike on the left with the specific reason on the right.

**1.** It helps fight pollution. _____
**2.** It helps you feel good. _____
**3.** It saves time. _____
**4.** It saves money. _____

**a.** You won't need to look for parking.
**b.** You won't burn gasoline.
**c.** You won't need to repair your car so often.
**d.** You'll get your daily exercise.

**12** Find the word in bold that means

   **a.** adds something _____   **b.** harms _____

# Small talk

## Vocabulary

**1** Look at the verbs and verb phrases in the box. Most have a negative connotation, or meaning, while the others are positive or neutral. Write the words in the correct columns.

| | | |
|---|---|---|
| ~~boring someone to tears~~ | bragging | chatting |
| complaining | confiding in someone | gossiping |
| making small talk | talking about someone behind his/her back | |

**Negative**

boring someone to tears

_____

_____

_____

_____

**Positive or neutral**

_____

_____

_____

**2** Match these conversation extracts with the verbs and verb phrases from Exercise 1.

1. So what have you been doing since I saw you last? I've missed talking to you and hearing about your life. _____chatting_____

2. It's a beautiful day, isn't it? _____

3. My daughter is the smartest child in her class. _____

4. Did you hear about the Langs? Their oldest son left college and is traveling around Europe. _____

5. I really hate my biology class. The teacher is always late, and he never explains anything in detail. _____

6. If I don't share this with someone, I'm going to explode. But if I tell you my big secret, do you promise not to tell anyone? _____

7. Luis told me he liked my new haircut, but then he turned around and told Anna that I looked like a French poodle. _____

8. It's nice that Hallie finally got a job she likes, but it's all she can talk about. Why does she think anyone really cares about all those details? _____

# Grammar ◀▬

**3**    **Match the statements with the tag questions.**

1. You're coming to the barbecue, _d_
2. You don't seriously mean that, _____
3. You won't be away next week, _____
4. John wouldn't mind if we started without him, _____
5. They've been working very hard, _____
6. He asked her out, _____
7. You couldn't leave the party early last night, _____
8. Paul lives in your neighborhood, _____
9. You bought that dress at The Rap, _____
10. That was a wonderful show, _____

a. didn't you?
b. wasn't it?
c. didn't he?
d. aren't you?
e. doesn't he?
f. do you?
g. haven't they?
h. will you?
i. could you?
j. would he?

**4**    **Complete the conversations with tag questions.**

1. **A:** That's not your dog, _is it?_
   **B:** Actually, yes. Why do you ask?

2. **A:** Mario won't be in Mexico this week, _____
   **B:** No, he's not going there until the 15th.

3. **A:** I know you, _____
   **B:** I don't think so.

4. **A:** There's a bank on this street, _____
   **B:** Yes. It's right on the corner.

5. **A:** Ivan and I are quitting our jobs and moving to Tahiti.
   **B:** You're kidding, _____

6. **A:** Sylvia has been acting strangely lately, _____
   **B:** Not really. She's always that way!

7. **A:** You wouldn't want to see a movie with me this weekend, _____
   **B:** I'd like nothing more!

8. **A:** That's an interesting building, _____
   **B:** *Interesting*? I'm not sure that's the word I'd use!

9. **A:** I will never again buy a used car.
   **B:** You had a bad experience with this one, _____

10. **A:** You don't like fish, _____
    **B:** It's not my favorite food, but I can eat it once in a while.

# 15

## Listening

**5** 🎧 **Play track 33. Listen to the five conversations. Answer the questions using short answers.**

**1. a.** On what day of the week does this conversation probably take place? *on a Monday*

    **b.** Did the man stay inside all weekend? _____

**2. a.** Is the man bragging or complaining? _____

    **b.** Is the woman interested in the man's description of his trip? _____

**3. a.** What have the people just done? _____

    **b.** Do they agree with each other? _____

**4. a.** Do you think the speakers know each other? _____

    **b.** Are the speakers bragging or confiding in each other? _____

**5. a.** What is the man talking about? _____

    **b.** Do you think the woman is interested in the conversation? _____

**6** 🎧 **Play track 33 again. Fill in the blanks. Write one word in each blank.**

**1.** The _____ _____ beautiful, _____ it?

**2.** It _____ usually _____ long, _____ it?

**3.** That movie _____ very good, _____ it?

**4.** That painting _____ awful, _____ it?

**5.** Times _____ changed, _____ they?

## Pronunciation

**7** Read the sentences aloud. Does the intonation of the tag question fall at the end (speaker is just asking for agreement)? Or does the intonation of the tag question rise at the end (speaker is asking a real question)? Take a guess and mark each question *F* (falling) or *R* (rising).

**1.** It's been fantastic weather, hasn't it?

**2.** It was a long trip, wasn't it?

**3.** They prepared all this food themselves, didn't they?

**4.** There isn't any more coffee, is there?

**5.** You don't happen to know where the restrooms are, do you?

**6.** She's in our English class, isn't she?

**7.** You will stay for dinner, won't you?

**8.** They couldn't have forgotten, could they?

**9.** You haven't met my husband yet, have you?

**10.** You work with computers, don't you?

**8** 🎧 **Play track 35. Notice the intonation and check your answers in Exercise 7. Then listen again and repeat.**

## Reading ◖▬

**9** Which of the following are good topics for small talk?

   **a.** hobbies _____     **b.** salary _____     **c.** travel _____     **d.** weather _____

**10** Read the article. What is the main idea?

   **a.** People make small talk when they have nothing to do.

   **b.** The topics in small talk should not be too serious.

   **c.** Small talk helps people build relationships.

**11** Write *T* (true) or *F* (false).

The author believes that people should not spend much time on small talk. _____

# Is Small Talk Really Small?

Small talk has nothing to do with size or importance. In fact, small talk is often the **foundation** for friendships and **solid** business relationships because it is a way to show **genuine** interest in another person and establish common **ground**. Small talk is like the warm-up to a full conversational workout.

Contrary to popular opinion, small talk is not "**idle** chatter" or a waste of time. It's better to take the time to connect with others, to discover the interests and opinions you share, than to save a little time. By avoiding small talk, you may be sending a message: "I don't want to waste my time finding out what your interests and preferences are."

What are good topics for small talk? In the US, weather tops the list—It affects everyone and there's always something to say about it. Light topics, such as sports, movies, pets, shopping, and fashion trends are good for striking up a conversation, especially if you know (or suspect) that the other person has some interest in the subject. Others are travel ("How was your trip?"); holidays ("Did you have a good break?"), and hobbies ("I hear you're a chess player.").

Which areas should generally be avoided in small talk? Politics, religion, romantic involvements, salary, age, weight, or other topics that may be viewed as too personal for **casual** conversation. It's also best to avoid complaining or gossiping, and never criticize your conversation partner during small talk.

Small talk is the way we build "big talk," so take it as seriously as any other kind of talk.

**12** Read the article again. Which of these questions would be appropriate for small talk?

   **a.** Nice and warm today, isn't it? _____

   **b.** How much do you make at your job? _____

   **c.** Have you been to the new shopping mall yet? _____

   **d.** Did you know that I used to date your girlfriend? _____

   **e.** You've put on some weight, haven't you? _____

**13** Find the word in bold that means

   **a.** informal _____    **b.** unproductive _____    **c.** basis _____

# A star is born ... or made?

## Vocabulary

**1** Complete the crossword puzzle.

The crossword grid contains the down answer at position 1: f a s h i o n a b l e, and position 8 begins with e.

**ACROSS**

3 liked by a lot of people

5 very interesting or exciting

7 modern and fashionable

8 neither good nor bad

9 very good at something that not everyone can do

**DOWN**

1 style, usually for a short period of time

2 very impressive and out of the ordinary

4 having a lot of power to affect someone's thoughts or actions

6 known or recognized by a lot of people

**2** Complete the article with the words from Exercise 1. Use each word only once.

This reporter was lucky enough to see one of the most **(1)** spectacular shows of the year. It was truly impressive. Victor Lara, a **(2)** _____ young singer, was the opening act for the **(3)** _____ performer Sandy Newton.

Victor isn't **(4)** _____ —at least, not yet! It won't take long for the world to know him. Victor's singing was absolutely **(5)** _____ —making Sandy's performance seem **(6)** _____ . Sorry, Sandy! The two entertainers' styles are similar—

Sandy has been very **(7)** _____ in the pop world for several years, with many younger performers naming him as their role model.

Dressed in **(8)** _____ jeans and a bright orange T-shirt, Victor Lara stole the show. The audience— supermodels and members of the entertainment community all dressed in **(9)** _____ clothes— went crazy and gave this newcomer a standing ovation as he left the stage. We'll see a lot more of this young singer.

# Grammar ◀━

**3** Complete the story with the appropriate passive form of the verbs in parentheses.

Stories about celebrities **(1)** _are published_ (**publish**) in newspapers and magazines. I usually don't pay much attention to them, but not long ago, I read an interesting story in one of my favorite magazines. A famous Las Vegas performer **(2)** _____ (**attack**) by a tiger during the show. The man **(3)** _____ (**take**) to a nearby hospital, where his injuries **(4)** _____ (**treat**). Several weeks later, the performer **(5)** _____ (**send**) to a rehabilitation center, where he **(6)** _____ (**keep**) for several months. I wonder what **(7)** _____ (**do**) to the tiger? I hope he **(8)** _____ (**not hurt**). Sometimes animals like lions and tigers that **(9)** _____ (**use**) for entertainment **(10)** _____ (**kill**) if people think they're dangerous. With luck, this one **(11)** _____ (**send**) back to Asia or wherever he came from originally.

**4** Rewrite the sentences in the passive, making any necessary changes. Use the agent only when needed.

1. When did they publish Madonna's first children's book?

   _When was Madonna's first children's book published?_

2. The wonderful artist Jeffrey Fulvimari drew the pictures for the book.

   _____

3. People recognize Madonna wherever she goes.

   _____

4. How much did they pay Tom Cruise for his last film?

   _____

5. Movie studios offer other actors a lot less money.

   _____

6. Gossip columnists often write about Tom Cruise.

   _____

7. In a recent interview, Cameron Diaz said her success overwhelmed her at first.

   _____

8. When Cameron Diaz was young, other children teased her a lot.

   _____

9. The other kids called her "Skinny Bones Jones" because she was very thin.

   _____

# 16

## Listening

**5** ⌒ Play track 37. Listen to the radio program about the Spice Girls. Why did each group member leave the group? Match the names with the reasons.

1. _____ Michelle

2. _____ Ginger Spice | left the group because she

3. _____ Posh Spice

a. got married.

b. wanted to go to college.

c. didn't get along with the others.

**6** ⌒ Play track 37 again. Fill in the blanks.

1. An advertisement _____ in a newspaper _____ a businessman.

2. Thousands apply, hundreds _____ , and five _____ eventually _____ .

3. Baby Spice, otherwise known as Emma Bunton, _____ to take her place.

4. Their first single, "Wannabe," _____ and becomes a huge success.

5. Ginger Spice leaves the group because of disagreements with the others, and _____ later _____ to be an ambassador by the _____ _____ .

## Pronunciation

**7** Read the adjective and noun pairs aloud. Underline the stressed syllable in each word.

1. fashionable    fashion
2. influential    influence
3. mediocre    mediocrity
4. popular    popularity
5. sensational    sensation

6. spectacular    spectacle
7. successful    success
8. talented    talent
9. trendy    trend

**8** ⌒ Play track 36. Listen to the pairs of adjectives and nouns. Check your answers in Exercise 7.

**9** ⌒ Play track 36 again. Listen and repeat.

# Reading

**10** What is an audition? Have you ever been on one?

**11** Read the article. Which would be the best title for this personal narrative?
   a. The Julliard School
   b. A Frustrating Experience
   c. An Unfair Process

**12** What is the main reason the writer is so interested in the Julliard School?
   a. It's in New York.
   b. Great actors studied there.
   c. It's very prestigious.

Well, today was my audition for Juilliard—one of the best places in the world to study acting, as well as music, art, and dance. It's in New York, right next to the Metropolitan Opera in Lincoln Center, and close to the theaters on Broadway. Many of its graduates, like Kevin Kline, Robin Williams, and Kelsey Grammer, moved on to spectacular acting careers.

The moment I walked into the hall where they were holding the audition, I realized I would be competing with more than 100 actors. It was horrible. After about an hour, we were divided into groups of ten, one group per hour, and given a time to audition. I was **relieved** that I was put in the first group. But it still took them another three hours to call me into the audition room.

Finally, the judges called me in and told me to sit in a chair facing them. After they asked me some basic questions, I began to perform my piece. I think I had their attention for about two minutes; after that, it was painfully obvious that they had stopped listening.

How could it be possible that my **fate** would be decided in just two minutes? I wanted to shout at them, to tell them how much I deserved to get in and how hard I had worked, but I didn't. I just thanked them and left the room. And sure enough, later in the day, they announced that, unfortunately, they wouldn't be calling anyone back.

It would be easy to give up my dreams and move on to something else. But I'd rather try to get into another—okay, less prestigious—school and make it my mission to show those judges what a mistake they made.

**13** Read the narrative again. According to the writer, if the aspiring actor performed poorly during the audition, the judges would
   a. tell the actor to stop and start again.
   b. let the actor finish and later reject him or her.
   c. stop the audition and call the next candidate.

**14** Underline the word closest in meaning to each of the words in bold.

   a. **relieved**:    comforted    released    unhappy
   b. **fate**:    good luck    destiny    career

# Self-Quiz for Units 13–16

## Vocabulary ⬤

### UNIT 13

**A** Write *S* if the words have the same or nearly the same meaning or *D* if they are different.

1. cut off / isolated __S__

2. fearful / stressed out _____

3. petrified / terrified _____

4. jumpy / jittery _____

5. solitary / lonely _____

6. isolated / tense _____

### UNIT 14

**B** Complete each expression with *time* with *a matter of, a waste of, by the, in, leisure,* or *take a long.*

1. She works two jobs, so she doesn't have a lot of ___leisure___ time.

2. The drive to the airport doesn't _____ time—only about an hour.

3. _____ time I got to the telephone, it had already stopped ringing.

4. Many people read or do work on the train so that their commute isn't _____ time.

5. It's just _____ time before Sara and Hector get married. Everyone knows that.

6. I set my alarm for 7:00 so I can be at the office _____ time for our 8:30 meeting.

### UNIT 15

**C** Underline the appropriate phrase to complete each sentence.

1. Don't just **complain** / **brag** about your situation—do something to change it!

2. It's good to have someone you can **gossip with** / **confide in** and share your deepest secrets with.

3. Mr. Blank knows everything about his neighbors. He loves to **gossip** / **make small talk** about them.

4. It is more productive to talk to someone directly than to **complain** / **talk behind their back**.

5. To **gossip** / **make small talk**, you can chat about the weather, sports, or famous actors!

6. It annoys me when Ricky **brags** / **makes small talk** about all the new things he buys. He has so much money.

### UNIT 16

**D** Underline the appropriate word to complete each sentence.

1. The magazines are showing the most **fashionable** / **mediocre** clothes of the season. This year it's bright colors and short skirts.

2. The senator is able to change the way a lot of people think. He is quite **influential** / **spectacular**.

3. The film was **sensational** / **talented**, and it received excellent reviews.

4. The owners of this **influential** / **trendy** shop sell only the latest and hottest clothes. You won't find any old styles here!

5. The band is very **popular** / **sensational** with teenagers; young girls especially like them.

6. Her music is **famous** / **influential** around the world. People in almost every country recognize her.

# Grammar

## UNIT 13

**(A)** Write the correct form of the verbs in parentheses to form present unreal conditional sentences.

1. If I _____ were _____ (be) you, I _would accept_ (accept) the job offer.

2. If the movie _____ (not be) so long, people _____ (enjoy) it more.

3. This room _____ (look) totally different if we _____ (paint) the walls.

4. What _____ you _____ (do) if you _____ (win) a million dollars?

5. If he _____ (train) really hard, he _____ (be able to) run the marathon.

6. You _____ (not feel) so stressed out if you _____ (plan) better.

## UNIT 14

**(B)** Rewrite the sentences using the words in parentheses. Make any necessary changes.

1. I left work early. However, I was late for dinner. **(although)**
   
   _Although I left work early, I was late for dinner._

2. In spite of the expense, she always visits her sister at least once a year. **(despite)**

3. He didn't know a lot of Spanish. However, he moved to Bolivia last year. **(in spite of)**

4. Although she doesn't like heights, she doesn't mind flying. **(despite not)**

5. The commute usually takes about 45 minutes, despite all the traffic. **(although)**

6. In spite of shopping a lot, Maria doesn't spend a lot of money. **(however)**

## UNIT 15

**(C)** Complete each statement with an appropriate tag question.

1. You don't have the time, _do you_? 
4. He won't tell her anything, _____?

2. He can drive me to work, _____? 
5. You were ready to go, _____?

3. You didn't forget her name, _____? 
6. They've already made dinner, _____?

## UNIT 16

**(D)** Complete the sentences with the passive form of the verbs in parentheses. Use the appropriate tense.

1. George Washington _was elected_ (elect) president of the United States in 1789.

2. The Beatles _____ (introduce) to many Americans in a 1964 TV appearance.

3. Popular stars _____ (interview) for magazines, television programs, and radio shows all the time.

4. This popular new wine _____ (import) from Chile.

5. About a billion Coca-Cola products _____ (consume) worldwide each day.

6. The audience _____ (entertain) by the spectacular singer's performance last weekend.

# What's in the fridge?

## Vocabulary

**1** Cross out the word that does not belong in each group.

1. beef     lamb     ~~salmon~~     veal

2. salami     nuts     pepperoni     ham

3. tuna     lobster     clams     mussels

4. snapper     shrimp     sole     tuna

5. popcorn     potato chips     crackers     roast beef

**2** Look at the puzzle and find five words that can be used to categorize the foods in Exercise 1. The words may go across (→) or down (↓).

```
A  S  L  M  C  L  P  B  O  T
E  I  D  R  O  K  U  H  X  Y
G  N  Q  U  L  E  Z  S  M  A
P  B  I  C  D  D  W  N  S  O
L  U  T  E  C  R  X  A  H  F
H  Y  S  G  U  D  I  C  W  I
O (M  E  A  T) P  Y  K  Z  S
L  N  B  F  S  U  J  S  R  H
S  E  A  F  O  O  D  K  R  C
```

**3** Match the words in the puzzle in Exercise 2 to the appropriate row in Exercise 1.

1. _____meat_____

2. _____

3. _____

4. _____

5. _____

## Grammar

**4** Circle the correct form of the verbs to complete the sentences.

1. I've decided (to take) / taking a cooking class.

2. These days, many people avoid **to eat** / **eating** meat.

3. Annie is going to give up **to drink** / **drinking** coffee.

4. So, did you manage **to get** / **getting** to the supermarket?

5. I'd offer **to make** / **making** dinner tonight, but I'm an awful cook!

6. Everyone is on a diet here, so I wasted my time **to make** / **making** dessert.

7. Josh and Nancy keep **to run into** / **running into** each other at the supermarket.

8. Are you planning **to cook** / **cooking** tonight, or should we go out for dinner?

9. We're having spaghetti and a salad tonight. We can't afford **to go out** / **going out**.

10. Why does Peter spend so much time **to read** / **reading** cookbooks when he never goes anywhere near the kitchen?

**5** Complete the article with the correct form—infinitive or gerund—of the verbs in parentheses.

# Simple Solutions for a *New* You

Try these fabulous ideas from our new health editor, Sarah Foster.

## A healthier you . . .

How are your eating habits? Do you keep on **(1)** _____saying_____ **(say)** you're going to start eating healthier food? We all try to avoid **(2)** _____ **(snack)** between meals, but we all do it. The next time you reach for a snack, avoid **(3)** _____ **(choose)** something sweet or salty. Have a piece of fruit! You'll feel better, too, if you decide **(4)** _____ **(exercise)** more. Don't just spend time **(5)** _____ **(talk)** about it. Join a gym and make sure you manage **(6)** _____ **(go)** there regularly.

## A happier you . . .

And how is your social life? Get out more. You probably waste a lot of time **(7)** _____ **(watch)** TV. Plan **(8)** _____ **(meet)** friends after work. Go somewhere you enjoy. And how about entertaining at home? Offer **(9)** _____ **(make)** dinner for a few close friends over the weekend. It doesn't have to be anything elaborate—the point is to spend time **(10)** _____ **(enjoy)** their company.

**17**

## Listening

**6** 🎧 Play track 40. Listen to Takanori Kotani, a chef from Japan. Answer the questions.

**1.** Why does Takanori want to get a new refrigerator?

_____

**2.** What does he usually have in his refrigerator?

_____

**3.** What kind of cheese does Takanori like? What kind of wine?

_____

**4.** Why is Takanori going to travel?

_____

**5.** What is he going to do when he's traveling? What isn't he going to do?

_____

**6.** What does Takanori do in his leisure time?

_____

**7** 🎧 Play track 40 again. Fill in the blanks.

**1.** You can't afford _____ _____ still in this business.

**2.** That's why I've decided _____ _____ other countries.

**3.** I won't waste time _____.

**4.** In fact, I hope _____ _____ some interesting new Thai and Chinese recipes.

**5.** I spend some of my free time _____!

## Pronunciation

**8** 🎧 Play track 69. Listen. Notice the pronunciation of the vowel sounds /i/ and /ɪ/. Write the words in the correct column.

| /i/ | /ɪ/ |
|---|---|
| eat | _____ |
| _____ | _____ |
| _____ | _____ |
| _____ | _____ |
| _____ | _____ |

**9** 🎧 Play track 69 again. Listen and repeat.

## Reading

**10** **Which of these types of food have you tried?**

Chinese _____      Mexican _____

Japanese _____      Middle Eastern _____

seafood _____      Korean _____

Italian _____      barbecue _____

**11** **Read the reviews. What type of food is served in each of the restaurants? Label them in the reading.**

## *Restaurant reviews*

 Golden Dynasty _____

This is a wonderful place for lunch. Food is excellently prepared with fresh ingredients. Every dish on the menu is **worth** trying, but my favorites are stir-fried beef with oyster sauce, Singapore noodles, and "Buddha's delight," a vegetable dish served with steamed rice. At lunchtime, they offer specials at great prices, and the service is fast and friendly. The portions are so large that a combination plate would be enough for two people. It's too bad the décor isn't more imaginative, but the hurried lunch crowd doesn't seem to mind.

 Dos Amigos _____

This is a family-owned restaurant that prepares all of their own food, including their famous tortilla chips. Burritos, tacos, fajitas, and enchiladas are very popular. There are several **meatless** vegetarian burritos, not just bean and cheese. Then there's the **mouth-watering** lobster burrito, my personal favorite. All the combination plates include refried beans and Mexican rice, with **abundant** portions that aren't **pricey** at all. The place looks rather ordinary, but don't be fooled: Everyone in the neighborhood knows about it and it gets crowded, so arrive early to avoid a long wait!

🦀 Beneath the Waves _____

**Situated** right on the harbor, this intimate dining spot is perfect for a romantic dinner. Popular dishes are BBQ jumbo shrimp, grilled mahi mahi, sautéed red snapper, and the spectacular steamed whole lobster. Steaks are also served, but they are not quite up to the standard of the other dishes. The place is **staffed** with gracious servers, although a bit slow, and the atmosphere is charming. Expect to pay for a fine dining experience that's well worth it.

**12** **Read the article again. Which restaurant would you choose if you . . .**

a. weren't worried about price? _____

b. were going there with a vegetarian? _____

c. wanted a very nice atmosphere? _____

d. didn't have much time? _____

**13** **Find the word in bold that means**

a. expensive _____     **b.** delicious _____     **c.** located _____

# Long walk to freedom

## Vocabulary

**1**    **Match the words with the definitions.**

    **1.** authorities  _d_

    **2.** cell _____

    **3.** guards _____

    **4.** life sentence _____

    **5.** political prisoner _____

    **6.** prisoner _____

    **7.** privileges _____

    **8.** supervision _____

    **a.** someone who is in prison as punishment for a crime

    **b.** people whose job is to prevent prisoners from escaping

    **c.** someone who is in prison for criticizing the government

    **d.** the people or organizations that are in charge of a particular place or people

    **e.** the punishment of being sent to prison for the rest of your life

    **f.** a small room in a police station or prison where prisoners are kept

    **g.** making sure others are behaving correctly

    **h.** special advantages given to one person or group of people

**2**    **Complete the articles with the words from Exercise 1.**

Prison **(1)** ___authorities___ have reported that convicted criminal Jacob Jones tried to escape last night and has been moved to a high-security prison in Texas. The **(2)** _____ will be kept in isolation in a small **(3)** _____ far from the other inmates. All of his **(4)** _____, such as time for exercise, have been taken away.

The political activist known simply as Veronica Y was released yesterday. Ms. Y was arrested in 1999 and found guilty of several crimes against the state. New evidence has proven her innocent. "When I was given a **(5)** _____, I knew I was going to spend the rest of my life as a **(6)** _____—even though I was innocent and had never done anything against the government. Now that I'm free, it feels wonderful not to be under constant **(7)** _____. There are no **(8)** _____ watching me anymore!"

# Grammar ◖▬▬

**3** Put the words in order to write sentences. Then look at the picture and match the sentences with the signs.

**1.** by / everyone / they / leave / midnight / made

*They made everyone leave by midnight.*
*Sign A*

**2.** anybody / they / let / gamble / didn't

**3.** inside / weren't / to / people / wear / boots / dirty / allowed

**4.** made / outside / guns / leave / their / they / cowboys / the

**5.** let / children / place / didn't / they / any / the / in / come

**6.** horses / their / cowboys / they / made / leave / the / outside

**4** Complete the article with the verbs in parentheses and the correct past form of *make, let,* or *be allowed to.* Add an object pronoun (*me, him, her,* etc.) where necessary.

**Reporter:** *Newsmonth* magazine _____*was allowed to speak*_____ to political activist Veronica Y
                                                **1. (speak)**

just before her recent release from prison. Thanks for agreeing to talk to us, Veronica.

Are you surprised that the authorities _____ you?
                                                        **2. (see)**

**Veronica:** I'm very surprised. Of course, they _____ not to say anything
                                                                **3. (promise)**

about the circumstances surrounding my possible release.

**Reporter:** Well, they _____ that we wouldn't talk about the years you've
                                **4. (promise)**

spent here. I hope you weren't treated badly.

**Veronica:** The most difficult thing was that my family _____ me the first
                                                                        **5. (visit)**

few years I was here. In fact, they _____ anyone from the
                                                **6. (see)**

outside. Finally, in 2002, friends and family _____ on
                                                            **7. (come)**

Sundays. The authorities _____ me food and small gifts, too.
                                        **8. (bring)**

The guards _____ them everything they were bringing in, but
                        **9. (show)**

they didn't mind.

# Listening

**5** 🎧 **Play track 41. Listen to the excerpt from Nelson Mandela's book. Change the incorrect word in each sentence.**

1. Mandela's prison cell was about ~~five~~ *six* feet wide.

2. He was 56 years old when he went to prison.

3. The work the prisoners did involved carrying stones.

4. The work was stressful and difficult.

5. The first week Mandela was in prison, he had only bread for lunch.

**6** 🎧 **Play track 41 again. Circle the words so that the sentences are true.**

1. The prisoners **were allowed / weren't allowed** to talk while working.

2. The guards **let / didn't let** the prisoners take a lunch break.

3. The prisoners **were allowed / weren't allowed** to exercise for more than half an hour a day.

4. The authorities **made / didn't make** the guards watch the prisoners while they exercised.

# Pronunciation

**7** 🎧 **Play track 42. Listen. Notice the weak pronunciation of the object pronouns and the way the pronouns are linked to the word before them. Fill in the missing words.**

1. They _____ *made us* _____ work in silence.

2. They _____ see our mail.

3. They _____ work all day on Sundays.

4. The guards _____ exercise.

5. They _____ write a letter every six months.

6. They _____ visit him often.

**8** 🎧 **Play track 42 again. Listen and repeat.**

## Reading 🔊

**9** What do you already know about Nelson Mandela?

**10** Read the quote at the beginning of the article. Is the statement below true or false? What word or phrase supports your opinion?

From Mandela's quote at the beginning of the article, you can tell that he was optimistic that he would see, in his lifetime, a democratic and free society in South Africa.

_____

> *"During my lifetime I have dedicated myself to the struggle of the African people. I have fought against white domination, and I have fought against black domination. I have cherished the ideal of a democratic and free society in which all persons live together in harmony and with equal opportunities. It is an ideal which I hope to live for and to achieve. But, if need be, it is an ideal for which I am prepared to die."*

Rolihlahla Mandela was born near Umtata, South Africa, on July 18, 1918. An indication of things to come, his first name could be translated to mean "troublemaker." On his first day of school, his teacher gave him the English name Nelson.

As a young man, Mandela joined a law firm in Johannesburg as an apprentice and, on a daily basis, witnessed the indignities of apartheid, which forced blacks to carry passes, kept blacks and whites separate, and legislated where blacks could live, work, and study.

The white minority in South Africa was in control of politics, the military, education, and most of the country's wealth. Mandela joined the Youth League of the African National Congress (A.N.C.) and became involved in programs of passive resistance against apartheid.

The government's response was to put Mandela and about 150 other activists on trial for treason. In 1961, after five years, they were acquitted. But the government banned all liberation movements, including the A.N.C., and Mandela went underground and traveled abroad to enlist support for the organization. It was for leaving the country that Mandela was arrested again in 1962 and ultimately given a life sentence to be served on Robben Island. While in prison, Mandela continued his education and his active involvement in the anti-apartheid cause. In 1990, then President F.W. de Klerk lifted the ban on the A.N.C. and announced Mandela's imminent release.

Mandela continued to work to unify a divided people and to bring democracy to South Africa. In 1993, Mandela was awarded the Nobel Peace Prize, and in 1994, apartheid officially ended and he was elected president of South Africa.

**11** Read the article. Put the events of Mandela's life in order (1–6) according to when they occurred.

_____ Nelson Mandela wins the Nobel Peace Prize.

_____ He joins a law firm as an apprentice.

_____ Mandela travels abroad without government's permission.

_____ Nelson Mandela is elected President of South Africa.

_____ Apartheid ends in South Africa.

_____ Mandela spends more than 25 years in prison.

**12** Find the words in paragraph 5 (The government's response . . .) that mean

**a.** prohibition _____  **b.** found innocent _____  **c.** cancelled _____

# Turning points

## Vocabulary

**1** Label the different types of reading material.

| advice column | encyclopedia | poetry / poems | anthology | textbook |
|---|---|---|---|---|
| ~~bestseller~~ | instruction manual | biography | novel | |

**In Our Time** #1 for more than 18 months!

**Important Safety Instructions**
1. Read and understand all instructions.
2. Follow all warnings marked on the product.

*Roses are red,*
*Violets are blue.*
*Sugar is sweet,*
*And so are you.*

1. _____bestseller_____   2. _____   3. _____

**Edgar Allan Poe (1809-1849)**

Edgar Allan Poe – poet, short-story writer, and literary critic – is one of the most important American writers of the 19th century. An orphan by the age of three, he was raised by a wealthy couple in Richmond, Virginia.

Report cards from the second semester were sent out soon after school closed in mid-June. Kennie's was a shock to the whole family. "If I didn't have to do so much work around the house..."

**THE BEST SHORT STORIES OF THE CENTURY**

4. _____   5. _____   6. _____

*Introduction to* **Biology**

**Guatemala** (GWAH·tuh·MAH·luh) has more people than any other country in Central America. Most of Guatemala's people live in the mountains in the central part of the country. Guatemala City is the capital and industrial center of Guatemala, and the largest city in Central America.

Dear Halley,
I've been dating a really nice guy for the past two months. We enjoy each other's company, and I like him a lot. The problem is that we never go out except to eat out. He never wants to go to clubs or the movies or parties. What should I do?

7. _____   8. _____   9. _____

# Grammar ◖

**2** Complete the conversations, using the verbs in parentheses in the past perfect or the past perfect continuous.

**1. Alice:** Why are you two so late?

   **Bob:** Well, when I got to Sam's house to pick him up, he still <u>hadn't gotten</u> **(not get)** dressed.

   **Sam:** I'm really sorry. When you rang the doorbell, I _____ **(stand)** in front of my closet for half an hour. I couldn't figure out what to wear!

**2. Hiroshi:** How was the movie last night?

   **Matt:** Oh, we didn't see it. By the time we got there, it _____ **(already/start)**. We were late because we _____ **(talk)** in the car. I guess we lost track of the time.

**3. Trina:** One of my favorite authors died yesterday. It says here that he _____ **(write)** stories since he was a child. By his twenty-first birthday, he _____ **(already/publish)** two novels.

   **Susan:** Amazing!

**3** Complete the biography with the past perfect or the past perfect continuous of the verbs in parentheses.

**Hemingway, Ernest (1899–1961),** was one of the most famous American writers of the twentieth century. He was born on July 21, 1899, in Oak Park, Illinois. He **(1)** _____ **(just/graduate)** from high school when he got a job as a reporter for a small newspaper. He **(2)** _____ **(work)** at the paper for less than a year when he signed up as a Red Cross volunteer. Hemingway served during World War I, which **(3)** _____ **(go on)** since 1914, and was sent to Italy in 1918. He **(4)** _____ **(drive)** a Red Cross ambulance for only six weeks when he was seriously wounded.

By 1921, Hemingway **(5)** _____ **(recover)** from his injuries and **(6)** _____ **(move)** to Paris. In Paris, he met several American writers who **(7)** _____ **(become)** known as the "Lost Generation" because of their bitterness caused by the war. When Hemingway returned to the United States in 1927, he **(8)** _____ **(already/write)** two of his most famous novels, *The Sun Also Rises* and *A Farewell to Arms.*

Before his death in 1961, Hemingway **(9)** _____ **(produce)** a large body of work. In 1986, Hemingway fans celebrated when *The Garden of Eden* was published. Hemingway **(10)** _____ **(write)** the novel before he died. He **(11)** _____ **(not complete)** it, but his publisher released it unfinished.

# 19

## Listening 🔊

**4** 🎧 **Play track 43. Listen to the radio program about actor Daniel Radcliffe. Write *T* (true) or *F* (false) next to each statement. Then correct the false statements.**

1. Daniel had always wanted to be an actor. __T__

2. Daniel's parents had always encouraged him to follow his dreams. _____

3. Daniel's big break had come with the first Harry Potter movie. _____

4. No one had heard of Daniel Radcliffe before the first Harry Potter movie came out. _____

**5** 🎧 **Play track 43 again. Check (✓) the things that are mentioned as Daniel's hobbies and interests.**

_____ clothes

__✓__ wrestling

_____ soccer

_____ skateboarding

_____ PlayStation games

_____ movies

_____ rock music

_____ dating

_____ auto racing

## Pronunciation 🔊

**6** 🎧 **Play track 44. Listen. Notice that *had* and *been* usually have weak pronunciations. Fill in the missing words.**

1. _She had_ always loved writing.

2. By the time she was six, _____ finished her first story.

3. _____ living in Portugal.

4. _____ a job teaching English.

5. _____ working on the book for a long time.

6. _____ a suitcase of stories.

**7** 🎧 **Play track 44 again. Listen and repeat.**

## Reading ◖◗

**8** Have you ever heard of Charles Dickens? What was his profession?

    **a.** actor         **b.** artist         **c.** journalist         **d.** novelist

**9** Read the article. *Oliver Twist* is

    **a.** an anthology         **b.** a biography         **c.** a novel

**10** Which stage of Dickens's life most influenced his writing? _____

# *Oliver Twist:* a classic for all times

Charles Dickens was one of the most popular writers of all time. He created some of the best-known characters in English literature. Born in England in 1812, he came from a poor family. His parents could not earn enough money to support their eight children, and Charles had to quit school at age twelve to find a job.

Determined to **break out of** a life of poverty, Dickens became a journalist and then a novelist. The difficulties the Dickens's family suffered and the **hopelessness** of his childhood **shaped** his view of the world and strongly influenced the subject matter and characters in his later writing. Many of his books concentrate on the connection between poverty and crime.

In one of his greatest books, *Oliver Twist*, Dickens **spoke out against** the terrible conditions of workhouses, where poor people were forced to live and work if they couldn't pay their debts. The story also painted a lively picture of London's criminal **underworld**, showing how the young and the weak were **forced into** a life of crime.

In the book, Oliver's mother died after giving birth to him, and he grew up in a workhouse, always hungry and cruelly treated. Oliver ran away to London, where he met a gang of young thieves who took him in. He tried to escape, but his past followed him. The **struggle** between good and evil becomes an exciting adventure, much loved by readers over the years.

**11** Read the article again. Write *T* (true) or *F* (false) after each statement.

    **1.** Charles Dickens grew up in a poor family. _____

    **2.** Dickens's parents were thieves. _____

    **3.** Dickens had great sympathy for the poor. _____

    **4.** *Oliver Twist* was the true story of Dickens's life. _____

**12** In *Oliver Twist*, Dickens describes the horrible conditions in London's

    **a.** prisons     **b.** poor families     **c.** workhouses

**13** Find the word or phrase in bold that means

    **a.** protested _____     **b.** long hard fight _____     **c.** influenced _____

# Looks good!

## Vocabulary

**1** Complete the crossword puzzle.

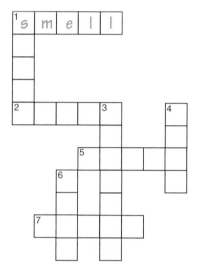

**Across**

1 What you do with your nose
2 What you do with your fingers
5 You do this with your mouth
7 Your perceive this with your ears

**Down**

1 Sense associated with your eyes
3 Sense associated with your ears
4 You do this with your skin, but most often with your hands
6 What you do with your eyes

**2** Complete the sentences with the correct form of verbs from Exercise 1. Use *like* when necessary.

1. We heard an awful noise outside. It _sounded like_ a cat fight.

2. Something _____ wonderful. Are you baking a cake?

3. Have you seen Jody's new sports car? It _____ something out of a James Bond movie!

4. The potatoes were delicious. They _____ the ones my grandmother used to make.

5. The baby's forehead _____ a little hot, so I took her temperature to make sure she didn't have a fever.

6. This blouse _____ silk. It's so smooth! But it's really polyester.

7. I spoke to Kathy on the phone today, and she _____ very excited about her trip to Mexico.

8. The milk _____ funny. I put a little in my coffee, and then I had to throw it away.

# Grammar

**3** Complete the sentences with a relative pronoun from the box. If the pronoun isn't necessary, put it in parentheses.

| that | when | where | where | which | who | whose |
|------|------|-------|-------|-------|-----|-------|

1. Did you like the perfume _(that)_ I gave you for your birthday last year?

2. It had a wonderful smell _____ reminded me of wildflowers.

3. This is the restaurant _____ Peter asked me to marry him.

4. I remember the time _____ he suggested we go dancing.

5. I had always wanted to meet someone _____ interests were similar to mine.

6. He's the funniest person _____ I know.

7. The hotel _____ we stayed offered swimming lessons every night in the pool.

**4** Combine the sentences. Add a relative pronoun if necessary, and make any other changes. More than one answer is possible in some cases.

1. I made a pie today. It tastes terrible.

   I made a pie today that tastes terrible.

2. We met an interesting couple last night. Their hobby is skydiving.

   _____

3. Please put the package in the office. Roberto works there.

   _____

4. There's an Indian movie on TV tonight. You might like it.

   _____

5. This is the time of year. I miss you the most.

   _____

6. Tom Cruise is a famous actor. He also produces movies.

   _____

7. I'm waiting for someone. You know him well.

   _____

## Listening 🎧

**5** 🎧 **Play track 45. Listen to the three commercials. What are they about? Complete the chart.**

|  | Fresh-and-White | Whisper | Port Royale |
|---|---|---|---|
| What is it? | toothpaste |  |  |
| Why should you buy it or go there? |  |  |  |

**6** 🎧 **Play track 45 again. Complete the sentences with the words you hear. You will not need to add anything in one sentence.**

1. Fresh-and-White was created with a unique and revolutionary formula _____ incorporates the best of nature.

2. If you're the type of person _____ likes to make an impact but in an ever-so-quiet way, Whisper is the perfume for you.

3. Experience the most delicate fragrance _____ you can imagine.

4. Are you looking for a place _____ you can relax and stay in touch with nature?

## Pronunciation 🎧

**7** 🎧 **Play track 46. Listen. Notice the pronunciation of the noun plurals and third-person singular present tense verbs. Fill in the blanks.**

1. It _____ like gentle rain.

2. My smile _____ white.

3. This _____ like mint.

4. Smell the _____.

5. Feel the _____.

6. It _____ like _____.

7. Bite into the sweet _____.

8. Watch the sun set from our white sandy _____.

9. Listen to the _____ of _____.

10. Enjoy the calming _____.

**8** 🎧 **Play track 46 again. Listen and repeat.**

# Reading

**9**    *Aromatherapy* is made up of two words: *aroma* and *therapy*. What is another word for each of these?

_____    _____

**10**    **Read the article. Write *T* (true) or *F* (false) next to each statement.**

a. Particular smells go directly to the ailing organs in our body. _____

b. Some aromatherapy oils could help people who get angry easily. _____

c. Aromatherapy is intended to help with some illnesses, but not to treat pain. _____

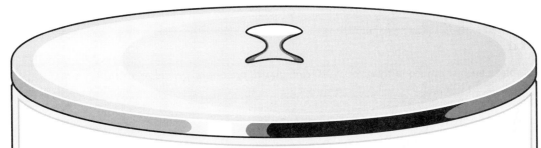

## AROMATHERAPY

Can you use your sense of smell to improve your health and **well-being**? Aromatherapists would argue that you most certainly can. Aromatherapy can be defined as the art of using "essential oils," the highly concentrated essences of aromatic plants, to heal the body and the mind. When people breathe in essential oils, the cells involved in smelling are stimulated and positive **impulses** are transmitted to the emotional center of the brain.

The essential oils used in aromatherapy are taken from different parts of plants with strong smells, such as the flowers, twigs, leaves, and bark, or from the rind of fruit. They can be blended in different combinations to treat a wide range of mental and physical problems. Essential oils can energize people or calm them down, so they can alleviate problems like anxiety, depression, fatigue, grief, irritability, loneliness, low **self-esteem**, nervousness, and stress. Aromatherapy can also help in the treatment of physical **ailments** like arthritis, asthma, skin problems, colds and flu, headaches, indigestion, toothaches, and burns.

Extracting these oils is very expensive and takes a considerable amount of time and expertise. The oils are very powerful and could cause injury if used alone. They are **diluted** before they are used in baths or massages or before they are **applied** to hair or skin.

Speaking of "diluted," aromatherapists are probably not too **pleased** to find that all sorts of household products—from dishwashing liquid to decorative candles—use the word "aromatherapy" on their packaging.

**11**    **Read the article again. Which of these is <u>not</u> a reason that aromatherapy works?**

a. Smells travel fast through the body.

b. There is a strong connection between mind and body.

c. Natural essences have healing properties.

**12**    **Find the word in bold that means**

a. the way you feel about yourself _____    c. made weaker _____

b. illnesses _____

# Self-Quiz for Units 17–20

## Vocabulary

### UNIT 17

**A** Circle the word in each group that is <u>not</u> an example of the category.

| | | | |
|---|---|---|---|
| 1. meat | (cheese) | beef | pork |
| 2. ingredients | sugar | salt | bake |
| 3. a meal | meat | dinner | breakfast |
| 4. seafood | shrimp | lobster | roast beef |
| 5. a snack | peanuts | sandwich | popcorn |
| 6. cold cuts | salami | ham | ice cream |

### UNIT 18

**B** Complete each sentence with *authorities, cell, guard, prisoners, privilege,* or *supervision*.

1. The ___prisoners___ are transported to the prison by bus.

2. My teenage daughter complains that her bedroom is as small as a _____.

3. We asked our neighbors twice to turn down the music before we called the _____.

4. The school makes sure there is always adult _____ for all after-school activities.

5. Voting should not be considered a _____, but a right.

6. A _____ protects the movie star's house. No one can enter without his permission.

### UNIT 19

**C** Match the words with the definitions.

1. a biography _f_   a. tells a fictional story

2. a bestseller ____   b. appears regularly in a newspaper or magazine

3. a manual ____   c. provides information about a school subject, such as science

4. a column ____   d. is popular with a lot of people

5. a novel ____   e. provides information about a machine or piece of equipment

6. a textbook ____   f. provides information about a person's life

### UNIT 20

**D** Complete each sentence with *feels, looks, smells, sounds,* or *tastes*. Add *like* when necessary.

1. This perfume is wonderful. It ___smells like___ a flower garden.

2. This scarf _____ so soft. It must be made of silk.

3. Dinner is delicious. Everything _____ so fresh!

4. The bride is so beautiful in her dress. She _____ a princess.

5. Listen to this CD. The group _____ the Beatles.

6. I don't know what's in the package, but it _____ a book when I pick it up.

# Grammar

## UNIT 17

**A** Complete each sentence with the gerund or infinitive form of *eat, fly, get, make, read,* or *run*.

1. Kerry avoids _eating_ in seafood restaurants because she doesn't like the smell.

2. If you give up _____ in the mornings, then how will you get your exercise?

3. She likes to spend time _____. Last weekend she finished two books!

4. I managed _____ Friday off from work, so we're going to beach for a long weekend.

5. We're planning _____ to Washington because the drive is too long.

6. She decided _____ a budget for herself. She's working on it right now.

## UNIT 18

**B** Complete the sentences with the appropriate form of the verbs in the parentheses.

a. He was __allowed to__ eat snacks at his grandparents' house. **(be allowed to)**

b. His parents _____ him do his homework before he could watch TV. **(make)**

c. The zoo workers _____ us touch the animals. **(not let)**

d. When I was a kid, my parents _____ me go to bed at a specific time. **(not make)**

e. The family always _____ the neighbors use their pool. **(let)**

f. My sister _____ to wear makeup until she was 16. **(not be allowed to)**

## UNIT 19

**C** Underline the appropriate verb to complete each sentence.

1. I **had been studying** / had studied for several hours when my friends came over.

2. She **had gone** / had been going to Acapulco once before.

3. When Bob arrived for the lecture, the speaker had talked / **had been talking** for over an hour.

4. The company **had been based** / was being based in Atlanta before it was moved to New York City.

5. The professor **hadn't read** / hadn't been reading the book's reviews before she bought it.

6. They hadn't been dating / **had dated** very long when Jack asked Michelle to marry him.

## UNIT 20

**D** Underline the word to complete each sentence.

1. This is the day **that** / when you've been waiting for!

2. This place reminds me of the restaurant **where** / that we had our first date.

3. I can't stand people **who** / which talk loudly on their cell phones.

4. A lot of tourists want to go someplace **where** / that has a lot of sunshine.

5. People which / **whose** cars are parked on the street after 11 A.M. will get tickets.

6. Hershey, Pennsylvania, is a town which / **where** is famous for its chocolate.

# Just looking

## Vocabulary

**1** Match the words with their definitions.

1. bait and switch _g_
2. coupon ___
3. exaggeration ___
4. fine print ___
5. loss leader ___
6. out of stock ___
7. package deal ___
8. rebate ___
9. warranty ___

a. an amount of money that is paid back to you, usually by mail

b. not available at the moment

c. a set of related things or services sold together

d. a written promise that a company will fix or replace something if it breaks after you have bought it

e. the details of a legal document, often in very small writing

f. a small piece of paper that you can use to pay less money for something or get it free

g. the practice of using bargain prices to attract customers and then trying to sell them higher-priced items

h. making something seem better, larger, worse, etc., than it really is

i. something sold at a lower price than normal in order to attract customers

**2** Read the training manual for employees at Better Buys, an electronics store. Complete the sentences with the correct form of words and phrases from Exercise 1.

> **Welcome to Better Buys!**
> **We have the best salespeople in town. Here's how to be one of them:**
>
> • Don't forget to point out a manufacturer's **(1)** ___rebate___. Customers love getting money back in the mail.
>
> • Encourage customers to keep their **(2)** _____. Some companies won't replace a broken item without it.
>
> • If a product that a customer wants is **(3)** _____, check the computer to see when it's expected to come in or whether it's available in one of our other stores.
>
> • Many people who come in because they saw that something was on sale will not have read the ad very carefully. If necessary, show them the ad, point out the **(4)** _____ (usually near the bottom), and explain it.
>
> • If a customer has a **(5)** _____, explain that this discount cannot be combined with any other offer.
>
> • Encourage customers to consider our **(6)** _____, and explain that they'll save money if they buy more than one thing at a time.

# Grammar

**3** Complete the sentences with the correct form of the verbs in the box. Use each verb once.

| be | ~~like~~ | use | visit | write |

1. Everyone in my family ___likes___ chocolate, so I buy it by the case because it's much cheaper.

2. Computers are so popular that nobody _____ typewriters anymore.

3. Because of email, no one _____ letters these days. It's a shame!

4. Anybody who _____ a mall will most probably buy something.

5. In the U.S., everything _____ on sale after the holidays.

**4** Complete the conversations with the appropriate indefinite pronoun. More than one answer is possible in some cases.

1. **A:** Ssh, the movie's already started. We don't want to bother ___anyone/anybody___.

   **B:** It's so dark in here, I can't see _____. How will we find a seat?

   **A:** Actually, we can sit anywhere we want. There's _____ here—except us. The theater is empty!

2. **A:** I'm dying for _____ sweet. Is there _____ sweet in the house?

   **B:** No, but why don't we make _____? How about cookies?

   **A:** That's a great idea. _____ likes cookies. Do we have the ingredients?

   **B:** Yes, I think we have _____ we need except eggs. _____ will have to run to the store.

   **A:** I'll go. Do we need _____ else?

   **B:** No, _____ else. That's it!

3. **A:** _____ says this store has the best prices in town.

   **B:** Well, I don't see _____ I like. Are you going to buy _____?

   **A:** No, I really don't need _____. Plus, _____ seems like a bargain here. _____ is much more expensive than at Better Buys.

*21*

## Listening

**5** 🎧 Play track 48. Listen to the two conversations between salespeople and customers. Circle the answer that correctly completes the sentences.

**Conversation 1**

1. The man is looking for a **CD player** / **DVD player**.

2. The store had advertised a model at **15 / 50** percent off.

3. The salesperson says she is going to show the customer a **better-quality / less expensive** model.

**Conversation 2**

4. The woman **is just looking / needs to buy a sofa as soon as possible**.

5. The salesperson doesn't say anything about the sofas' **quality / comfort**.

6. According to the salesperson, the sale ends **today / tomorrow**.

**6** 🎧 Play track 48 again. Which sentence do you hear? Listen and circle *a* or *b*.

1. a. Is there anything I can help you with?
   b. Is there something I can help you with?

2. a. Is there anything in particular you're looking for?
   b. Is there something in particular you're looking for?

3. a. Everyone is raving about them.
   b. Everybody is raving about them.

4. a. No one has returned any of these sofas yet!
   b. Nobody has returned any of these sofas yet!

## Pronunciation

**7** 🎧 Play track 49. Listen. Notice the stress in the indefinite pronouns. Underline the part of the pronoun that has the stress.

1. <u>Every</u>one loves these.

2. No one has returned them.

3. Would you like something to drink?

4. I'm afraid there's nothing I can do.

5. Everybody is raving about them.

6. You won't find anything like it.

**8** 🎧 Play track 49 again. Listen and repeat.

# Reading

**9** Which of these things should you think about when you shop on the Internet?

    **a.** pickpockets ___    **b.** privacy ___    **c.** refund policies ___

    **d.** security ___    **e.** shipping costs ___    **f.** store hours ___

**10** Read the article. Match each of these statements with the correct tip from the article.

    **a.** "When will the package be delivered to me?" ___

    **b.** "I'm afraid I can't give you my password." ___

    **c.** "The symbol of a key means it's a safe website." ___

    **d.** "Where did I put that order number?" ___

## Cyber-smart tips for shopping online

Nowadays, you can purchase almost anything on the Internet, 24 hours a day, 7 days a week. But before you do, here are some tips:

**1 Know the merchant.** It's best to do business with companies you already know, but if the seller is new to you, you might start with a small order as a **trial**.

**2 Shop at secure websites.** How can you tell if a website is secure? The order form should display the letters "https" at the top of the screen. The letter s means it is a secure site that **scrambles** your information, such as a credit card number, so it can't be stolen. Also, look for icons of a lock, padlock, or key at the bottom of the screen.

**3 Guard your privacy.** Be careful when online **merchants** ask for personal information. You don't have to **disclose** it, especially when you don't know how it will be used. Also, some websites ask you to create a password. If someone asks you for your password, never give it out.

**4 Get details.** Find out other information related to your **purchases**. For example, how long does shipping take and who pays for it? Can you return the item for a full refund if you're not satisfied? Policies should be stated on the website, but if you're not sure, don't hesitate to call.

**5 Keep records.** Print out the order **confirmation** or store it on your computer. You may need it later in case of problems.

**11** Read the article again. Which one of these symbols shows you that a website is secure?

    **a.**    **b.**    **c.**

**12** Name three things you should find out before buying something online.

    _____   _____   _____

**13** Find the word in bold that means

    **a.** sellers _____    **b.** mixes up _____    **c.** a test _____

# Shaking hands

## Vocabulary

**1** Cross out the word or phrase that does not usually go with the verb on the left.

| | | | |
|---|---|---|---|
| **1.** do | ~~a meeting~~ | a good job | business with someone |
| **2.** make | contact | business | an appointment |
| **3.** reach | an agreement | a destination | contact |
| **4.** set up | an appointment | an agreement | a meeting |
| **5.** take | care of something | a risk | a deal |
| **6.** schedule | a meeting | an appointment | an agreement |
| **7.** negotiate | a reasonable price | an appointment | a good deal |
| **8.** consult | the sales reps | a business trip | a supervisor |
| **9.** exchange | business meetings | telephone numbers | business cards |
| **10.** go | on a trip | in a meeting | to an appointment |

**2** Read the email a businessman sent to a colleague. Complete the message with the appropriate form of the verbs from Exercise 1. You will not need all of them. More than one answer is possible in some cases.

John,

I've been selling paper for a long time, and I've **(1)** __gone__ on hundreds of business trips, but this one is a bit stressful because the price of paper is very high right now. Our company **(2)** _____ a lot of business here with many of the large publishers.

I always call ahead to **(3)** _____ appointments with the people in charge of buying paper for their company. Today, I **(4)** _____ a risk, however, and popped in on a new client without calling to **(5)** _____ a meeting. Fortunately he was free, and he agreed to see me.

After discussing the company's needs, we were able to **(6)** _____ an agreement about the size of their first order. We went back and forth, and he **(7)** _____ with his boss. Finally we **(8)** _____ a deal that made everyone happy. Before leaving the office, we **(9)** _____ business cards and I promised to call them as soon as the order was placed at our factory.

## Grammar 

**3** Read the first sentence. Then mark each sentence below it *T* (true) or *F* (false).

**1.** If Louis lived downtown, he wouldn't have to drive to work every day.

   **a.** Louis lives downtown. _F_

   **b.** Louis drives to work every day. ___

**2.** I'd call the office if I had a cell phone.

   **a.** I'm about to call the office. ___

   **b.** I have a cell phone. ___

**3.** If Mona's new client places a large order, she'll get a raise.

   **a.** Mona's client has placed a large order. ___

   **b.** Mona might get a raise. ___

**4** Write future real conditional or present unreal conditional sentences about the situations.

**1.** The meeting will probably end late. I want to take a taxi home.

   If the meeting ends late, I'll take a taxi home.

**2.** It's likely that I'll get a raise next week. I'm going to buy a new TV.

**3.** We want to increase our sales, but we need to have a website.

**4.** The owner doesn't want to sell the company. He doesn't want his employees to lose their jobs.

**5.** I want to go to work today, but I feel really sick.

**6.** I'm sure we'll reach an agreement soon. I don't want to have to work this weekend.

**7.** He wants to write to her, but he doesn't know her email address.

**8.** You don't take any risks. You're not more successful.

107

## Listening

**5**   Play track 50. Listen to part of an interview with a business consultant. Match the countries with each description.

| Argentina    the U.K.    Spain    ~~Turkey~~    the U.S. |

1. Business interactions here don't go quickly. ___Turkey___

2. A business dinner in this country will start at a later hour than most people are accustomed to. _____

3. A business lunch here might be held in a pub. _____

4. Business lunches here are usually relaxed. _____

5. Business lunches here don't usually last very long.

   _____

**6**   Play track 50 again. Which sentence do you hear? Listen and circle *a* or *b*.

1. a.  You probably won't have so many cross-cultural problems if you travel close to home.

   b.  You probably wouldn't have so many cross-cultural problems if you traveled close to home.

2. a.  If I visit an office there, they will almost certainly offer me a hot drink.

   b.  If I visited an office there, they would almost certainly offer me a hot drink.

3. a.  I'll be prepared to have a long meeting if I want to negotiate a deal there.

   b.  I would be prepared to have a long meeting if I wanted to negotiate a deal there.

4. a.  If you're invited out to dinner, it probably won't start until 9:00 or 10:00 P.M.

   b.  If you were invited out to dinner, it probably wouldn't start until 9:00 or 10:00 P.M.

## Pronunciation

**7**   Play track 51. Listen. Notice the intonation in these conditional sentences. Underline the two words that receive the main stress in each sentence.

1. If you give someone a <u>gift</u>, you should use both <u>hands</u>.

2. If I visited an office, they would offer me a hot drink.

3. If you have a business lunch, it will be leisurely and relaxed.

4. If you kept an executive waiting, it would be an insult.

**8**   Play track 51 again. Listen and repeat.

# Reading

**9** What is jet lag?

_____

**10** Read the article. Which statement is true about jet lag?

a. Jet lag occurs when you travel late at night.

b. There is no single real remedy for jet lag.

c. Jet lag is basically a psychological disorder.

HAVE YOU EVER FLOWN ACROSS several time zones, like going from London to New York or from Mexico to Hawaii? If you have, you probably know that uncomfortable feeling called "jet lag." At one moment, you may feel really tired, and at another moment, full of energy. According to various international studies, almost everyone on a long flight suffers jet lag to some degree.

Jet lag is basically a sleep **disorder**. It **results** when a person's internal clock tries to get accustomed to a new external environment. This **acclimatization** involves circadian rhythms, or changes in the body that occur throughout a 24-hour period, such as **fluctuations** in your body temperature and the **urge** to fall asleep. When you cross several time zones in a short period of time, your circadian rhythms cannot adjust quickly enough.

How can you **combat** jet lag? Different people **subscribe to** different "remedies," such as following a certain diet for a time before you travel, using herbal medicines, or undergoing light therapy, but there is no real cure. Here are some common-sense suggestions:

- Get a good night's sleep the night before your flight.
- Get plenty of exercise in the days prior to your departure.
- Drink water, but **avoid** soft drinks, coffee, tea, juice, and alcohol, especially.
- Get up and walk around during the flight.
- Use blindfolds, ear plugs, neckrests, and blow-up pillows to help you get quality sleep during the flight.
- If possible, get fresh air and sunlight after you arrive at your destination.

**11** Read the article again. Which statement best explains why a person traveling from Chicago to Mexico City would probably <u>not</u> experience jet lag? (All statements are true.)

a. It takes about 4 hours to travel between both cities.

b. Both cities are in the same continent.

c. Both cities are in almost the same time zone.

**12** All of the following remedies are mentioned in the article <u>except</u>

a. taking herbal remedies

b. using magnets

c. changing sleep patterns

**13** Find the word in bold that means

a. changes _____  b. desire _____  c. follow _____

# Growing up

## Vocabulary

**1** Write the words and phrases in the box under the correct categories. Write one word only in each category. Then add an idea of your own to each category.

| | | | |
|---|---|---|---|
| birthdays | calling names | getting married | good friends |
| ~~not doing homework~~ stories | | teachers | strict |

Things kids might try to "get away with"

_____*not doing homework*_____

_____

People we "look up to"

_____

_____

Things kids do to "pick on" one another

_____

_____

Important issues we "think over"

_____

_____

Things we "make up"

_____

_____

People we "count on"

_____

_____

Things we "look forward to"

_____

_____

The way some parents are about "bringing up" their kids

_____

_____

**2** Read the advice from a parenting expert. Complete the sentences with the correct form of the phrasal verbs in quotations in Exercise 1.

Everyone knows how hard it is to (1) ___*bring up*___ kids these days. Many child psychologists feel that part of the problem comes from the fact that we let our children (2) _____ too much. Do we? Is it a bad idea to look the other way every once in a while? When kids (3) _____ stories that turn out to be lies, should they be punished? It depends on the seriousness of the situation. (4) _____ the appropriate and fair punishment for your children's behavior before you decide on what to do about it. Your children

(5)_____ you and need to know that they can (6) _____ you to support and understand them. Talk to your kids. Ask lots of questions. Is anyone (7) _____ them at school? Children can be incredibly cruel to one another. Kids who are being verbally abused (what hurts more than unkind words?) won't (8) _____ going to school and run the risk of doing badly in their classes. We need to make school a positive experience if we want our children to succeed.

# Grammar ◖▬

**3** Which of the phrasal verbs in the box are separable (the object can go between the verb and the particle)? Which are inseparable (the object must go after the particle)? Write them in the correct columns.

| | | | |
|---|---|---|---|
| ~~bring up~~ | count on | figure out | get away with |
| look forward to | look up to | make up | pick on |
| put up with | think over | turn into | |

| Separable | Inseparable |
|---|---|
| bring up | |

**4** Complete the conversations with the correct forms of the words in parentheses.

1. **Anne:** Mom! Steven won't stop _picking on me_ (pick on/me)!

   **Mother:** Steven, why are you being so mean to your little sister? You know she _____ (look up to/you).

   **Steve:** I don't care, Mom. She's bothering me, and I don't know why I have to _____ (put up with/it) just because I'm older.

2. **Paula:** I thought Paul liked me, but lately he hardly talks to me. I can't _____ (figure out/him).

   **Karen:** That's too bad. I know you _____ (count on/him) to take you to the dance next month. Why don't you ask him what's wrong?

   **Paula:** Do you think I should do that? Hmm. Let me _____ (think over/it).

3. **Kioko:** What kind of child were you, Jenna?

   **Jenna:** Pretty normal. My parents weren't very strict, but they didn't let my brother and me _____ (get away with/much). They _____ (bring up/us) to respect others and to believe in ourselves.

   **Kioko:** Well, I _____ (look forward to/meeting) your family.

4. **Raul:** Did you use to get in trouble a lot when you were a kid?

   **Alex:** Not really. Every time I did something bad, like missing homework I'd _____ (make up/something) that got me out of trouble. I was really good at that.

   **Raul:** Maybe that's why you _____ (turn into/a marketing genius)!

## Listening

**5** Play track 52. Listen to someone talk about growing up. Circle the answer that correctly completes the sentences.

1. The speaker got in trouble a lot when he was about **fourteen / nineteen**.

2. His friends **got / didn't get** punished a lot.

3. He **was / wasn't** punished a lot.

4. The young man and his parents **have / don't have** a good relationship now.

5. He **used to / didn't use to** admire his parents very much.

**6** Play track 52 again. Fill in the blanks.

1. Even though they tried to _____ _____ _____ right, I was always getting into trouble.

2. My friends and I used to be terrible in school—always _____ _____ the younger kids.

3. Somehow my friends always seemed to _____ _____ _____ stuff.

4. I don't know how my parents _____ _____ _____ _____.

5. I _____ _____ _____ them very well now that I'm a little bit older.

6. I actually _____ _____ _____ them more now than when I was a kid.

## Pronunciation

**7** Play track 53. Listen. Notice the stress in the phrasal verbs. Underline the part of the verb that has the stress.

1. Growing <u>up</u> is figuring things <u>out</u> for yourself.

2. Don't believe that. He probably made it up.

3. I don't know how my parents put up with me.

4. I get along with them well now.

5. I knew I could count on her.

6. We used to pick on them.

**8** Play track 53 again. Listen and repeat.

112

# Reading ◖▬▬

**9** Birth order refers to children's positions in a family based on who was born first, second, etc. Which of these things do you think could be affected by birth order?

achievements ___     friendships ___     hair color ___     occupation ___     abilities ___

**10** Read the article. What is the best title?

**a.** Growing Up With Siblings

**b.** Personality and Birth Order

**c.** Problems of the Only Child

EACH CHILD IN A FAMILY HAS a distinct personality. But did you know that birth order can affect personality traits and may even be related to a person's choice of occupation and ability to form social relationships?

**The first-born** is often a natural leader who is dependable, self-confident, and conscientious. First-borns also tend to be perfectionists who try to achieve their best. Over half the U.S. presidents have been first-borns.

**The only child** is much like the first-born— dependable and conscientious. Because they grow up alone, they may have weak social skills and can sometimes be self-centered. Their feelings are easily hurt, and they tend to be loners.

**The middle child** may feel overshadowed in the family by the first-born or the last-born. They sometimes feel they have no place in the family, so friendships are important. They are often sociable and do well at team sports. They are often entrepreneurs and work for themselves.

**The last-born** ("the baby of the family") tends to be outgoing and sociable. Because they yearn for attention from parents and older siblings (brothers and sisters), they can be charming and funny, but they can also be spoiled, self-centered, and rebellious. Often they are people-oriented, so they make good salespeople. Many writers are also last-borns.

As you would expect, there are exceptions. For example, when there are more than five years between the first and second child, the second may resemble a first-born. Natural differences in personality, gender, and physical appearance come into play as well.

What is your own birth order? Are the descriptions accurate for you, your friends, and your family members?

**11** Read the article again. Based on the information in the article, which child is most likely to become

**a.** the president of a large company? _____

**b.** a salesperson? _____

**c.** a business owner? _____

**12** Label these adjectives positive (+) or negative (−).

charming ____          conscientious ____          dependable ____

outgoing ____          rebellious ____          self-centered ____

self-confident ____          sociable ____          spoiled ____

# Neat and clean

## Vocabulary

**1** Complete the crossword puzzle.

```
                                              3 □
                                                □
        1 o        2 □                           □
          r          □                           □
          g          □                           □
4 □       a      5 □ □ □ □ □ □                    □
  □       n          □
  □       i          □
  □       z          □
  □     6 e □ □ □ □ □ □ □ □ □
  □       □          □
7 □ □ □ □ □ □ □ □     □
  □
```

**Across**

**5** If we have a party and don't want to do all the work ourselves, we can hire someone to _____ it.

**6** Many stores offer to do this for free so their customers don't have to carry heavy bags.

**7** When we use a device to make clothes smooth, we're doing the _____.

**Down**

**1** When we plan or arrange something, we _____ it.

**2** New computer software has to be _____ before it can be used.

**3** We go to the supermarket to do the _____ shopping.

**4** When we dust, vacuum, and scrub, we're doing _____.

**5** When we prepare meals, we're doing the _____.

**2** Which words and phrases related to household chores usually go with *do*? Write five from Exercise 1 and one more of your own.

Do — the grocery shopping

# Grammar

**3** Complete these sentences with the appropriate reflexive pronoun.

**1.** I'm not doing your homework for you. You have to do it <u>yourself</u>.

**2.** Pablo cut _____ while he was shaving this morning.

**3.** The lights are on a special timer. They automatically turn _____ on when it gets dark.

**4.** With four children, it must be hard for you and Abby to find time for _____.

**5.** Sharon treated _____ to a poetry book for her birthday.

**6.** Nobody invited us to the party. We invited _____.

**4** Sally and Rick have just moved into an old house that needs a lot of work. Sally has ideas about what to do, but Rick reminds her that they can't afford it. Use the cues to write their conversation.

**1. (the house/paint)**

Sally: <u>Let's have the house painted.</u>

Rick: <u>We can't afford to have it painted. We should paint it ourselves.</u>

**2. (the roof/repair)**

Sally: Why don't we _____?

Rick: Let's _____.

**3. (flowers/plant)**

Sally: We should _____.

Rick: How about we _____?

**4. (the windows/wash)**

Sally: Let's _____.

Rick: Why don't we _____?

**5. (a new dishwasher/install)**

Sally: We should _____.

Rick: We could also _____.

# Listening

**5** ⌒ Play track 54. Listen to people talk about things they need to do. Underline the choice that correctly completes the sentences.

**Conversation 1**

1. The woman's problem is that she's having a difficult time **going to the supermarket** / cooking.

2. The woman's daughter suggests she **hire a service to do the food shopping / have her meals delivered.**

**Conversation 2**

3. The man and woman are Lemar's **parents / grandparents.**

4. The man and woman can't do the shopping and preparation because they **live too far from the supermarket / don't have time.**

**6** ⌒ Play track 54 again. What will the people probably say next?

**Conversation 1**

The daughter will probably say "What about _____

a. having your grocery shopping done by a service?"

b. you do the shopping yourself and hire someone to cook?"

**Conversation 2**

The husband will probably say, "Let's _____

a. have the party catered."

b. have the groceries delivered to our door."

# Pronunciation

**7** ⌒ Play track 56. Notice the way the focus word in each sentence or clause stands out. Underline the focus word(s) in each sentence.

1. **A:** Would you ever have your <u>laundry</u> done for you?
   **B:** No, I'd rather do it <u>myself.</u>

2. **A:** Did you have your hair cut at the corner salon? It looks nice!
   **B:** I cut it myself. Thanks.

3. **A:** My car is really dirty, but I don't want to wash it myself.
   **B:** Why don't you have it washed at that new car wash? They're great!

4. **A:** My bike is broken. I usually repair it myself, but I don't have time.
   **B:** I had mine repaired at The Spoke Shop last week. They did a good job.

5. **A:** Did you have your house painted? The new colors look great.
   **B:** Actually, we painted it ourselves. We did it during our vacation.

6. **A:** Do you have gifts wrapped when you buy them at a department store?.
   **B:** Only if there's no extra charge. Otherwise, I wrap them myself.

**8** ⌒ Play track 56 again. Listen and repeat.

# Reading

**9** **What do you think a *pack rat* is?**

a. a person who carries a lot of bags

b. a person who likes to hike

c. a person who never throws anything away

**10** **Read the article. What is the main topic?**

a. people who are messy

b. professionals who can help you get organized

c. techniques to cure chronic disorganization

# Time to Get Organized

It's the newest trend. Add it to the list of other in-home personal services. Did you know that there is a professional organization that can help you if you feel completely overwhelmed by the amount of **clutter** in your living space? Now you can hire someone to come to your home and help you organize. It's the perfect solution for the pack rat—the person who **hoards** every scrap of paper or **can't bear** to part with an old cardboard box.

Judith Kolber is the founder of the National Study Group on Chronic Disorganization (NSGCD), an organization of professional organizers. The NSGCD has a certificate program for people who want to become professional organizers. It also helps disorganized people get organized by providing telephone **coaching** or **referrals** to a personal organizer. The NSGCD takes chronic disorganization very seriously.

If you believe you are among the chronically disorganized, you can take a 21-question questionnaire on their website to measure your level of disorganization.

Here is a short version of the CD (chronic disorganization) questionnaire.

1. Are you a collector (books, postcards, model cars, etc.)?

2. Are you the type of person who loses track of time and misplaces things?

3. Does it take you more than a few minutes to find important papers on your desk?

4. Do you shop all the time? Are you a shopaholic?

5. Is your desk or floor covered with books, receipts, and papers?

6. Are you ever embarrassed to invite friends to your place because it's messy?

7. Are you a pack rat?

If you answered YES to five or more questions, you probably have CD. Maybe it's time for you to contact a professional organizer.

**11** **Read the article again. Which of the following is <u>not</u> mentioned as a way that NSGCD helps people who are chronically disorganized?**

a. a referral to a professional    b. a special questionnaire    c. psychological counseling

**12** **Which of the following statements might be made by a chronically disorganized person?**

A place for everything and everything in its place.

I don't have time to put things away.

I'm totally overwhelmed by all this clutter.

If you're done with it, put it away.

You never know when you might need that!

I might be able to fit one more thing in that corner over there.

**13** **Find the word in bold that means**

a. advice _____    b. keeps _____    c. refuses _____

117

# Self-Quiz for Units 21–24

## Vocabulary

### UNIT 21

**A** Match the words with the advertising examples.

**1.** a coupon  *b*

**2.** bait and switch _____

**3.** a package deal _____

**4.** a warranty _____

**5.** an exaggeration _____

**6.** a rebate _____

**a.** This product will change your life!

**b.** Cut here and save 75¢ on your next purchase of Brite toothpaste!

**c.** Send in your receipt and receive $25 back!

**d.** We're out of that item, but we have a better version for only $20 more!

**e.** Buy the complete set of tools and save $30.

**f.** If the item breaks within two years of purchase, we'll replace it.

### UNIT 22

**B** Underline the word that goes with the verb.

**1.** make  <u>contact</u> / risks / business

**2.** set up  an appointment / a sales rep / business cards

**3.** reach  an agreement / an appointment / a business trip

**4.** take  a business / an agreement / risks

**5.** negotiate  a meeting / a deal / an appointment

**6.** exchange  risks / business cards / meetings

### UNIT 23

**C** Complete each sentence with *count on, get away with, look forward to, look up to, pick on,* or *think over*.

**1.** If the lawyers can't prove this man is guilty, then he's going to <u>get away with</u> the crime.

**2.** Children often _____ famous people and try to be like them.

**3.** She's going to _____ all her options before she makes a decision.

**4.** You can _____ me to help you. I'll do whatever you need.

**5.** I'm so excited about our family party. I always _____ seeing everyone.

**6.** David comes home crying every day because some kids _____ him at school.

### UNIT 24

**D** Underline the word to complete each sentence.

**1.** The hotel **delivered / served** the newspaper to us every morning.

**2.** When do you usually **do / organize** the housework?

**3.** You can hire someone to **do / cater** the party so you don't have to cook.

**4.** After water leaked all over the floor, plumbers came to **fix / deliver** the broken pipe.

**5.** If you **fix / organize** the files, you'll be able to find things a lot more easily.

**6.** It's best to **serve / cater** the food as soon as you finish cooking so it doesn't get cold.

# Grammar

## UNIT 21

**A**  Complete each sentence with *anyone, anything, everybody, everything, no one,* or *something.*

1. They don't have ___anything___ to do on Saturday night.

2. _____ is on the table for dinner except the main dish.

3. _____ seems to know anything about the product.

4. I haven't spoken to _____ about it.

5. _____ wants to do something to help.

6. Here's _____ you can read on the plane.

## UNIT 22

**B**  Form future real conditional or present unreal conditional with the appropriate form of the verbs in parentheses.

1. The meeting may finish early. If it ___is___ (be) over by 6:00, he __will give__ (give) us a call.

2. It's rush hour now. If you _____ (take) the car, you _____ (get) stuck in traffic.

3. She _____ (make) fewer mistakes if she _____ (listen) to me, but she doesn't.

4. We never have money to travel. If we _____ (be) rich, we _____ (take) a trip to Europe.

5. He's never home. His kids _____ (love) it if he _____ (work) less.

6. Let's make a deal. If you _____ (buy) the car now, I _____ (take) $1,000 off the price.

## UNIT 23

**C**  Complete the sentences with the appropriate form of the phrasal verbs + object in parentheses.

1. If you can't ___figure it out___, let me know and I'll help you. **(figure out/it)**

2. Sally was always _____ younger brother and making him cry. **(pick on/her younger brother)**

3. Don't _____. Tell me what really happened.  **(make up/things)**

4. Her parents work a lot, so her grandparents are really _____. **(bring up/her)**

5. Kids _____ to teach them a lot of things. **(count on/their parents)**

6. We needed to _____ before we made a decision. **(think over/the options)**

## UNIT 24

**D**  Complete the sentences with a passive causative or a reflexive pronoun. Use the cues in parentheses.

1. Let's ___have the car washed___ (car/wash). It looks nice when a professional does it.

2. Even if I were rich, I would _____ (do/cooking) because I enjoy it.

3. I'm _____ (cater/party). It's too much work for one person.

4. She likes _____ (wash/dishes). She says that it's relaxing.

5. You can _____ (deliver/groceries). The supermarket does it at no extra charge.

6. I decided to _____ (cut/hair). I can't afford the high prices anymore.

# A winning formula

## Vocabulary

**1** Find nine words related to business processes. The words may go across (→) or down (↓).

```
H  U  P  L  A  N  R  Z  Q  M
B  S  R  T  D  L  I  B  A  A
U  P  O  U  V  K  Y  Z  G  R
S  R  D  B  E  X  S  T  Y  K
I  O  U  P  R  O  D  U  C  E
N  F  C  E  T  M  V  H  N  T
E  I  T  X  I (A  D) Z  R  V
S  T  Q  Z  S  Y  K  H  J  U
S  A  B  D  E  S  I  G  N  W
```

**2** Complete the article with the correct form of the words from Exercise 1.

Imagine that you own a company that **(1)** _produces_ soft drinks—juices and sodas. Your goal is to make money, but how will you make a **(2)** _____? How will you sell your **(3)** _____? It's not easy to do **(4)** _____ these days, but many companies are successful at selling us the things they want us to buy.

First, think about your largest **(5)** _____: who drinks the most soda and juice? Probably teenagers. So you need to **(6)** _____ in places where teenagers go—by running **(7)** _____ in teen magazines, for example, and commercials during TV shows that are popular among teens.

The appearance of things helps—or hurts—their appeal. The **(8)** _____ should be exciting: It is a fact that people often buy something because they like the package. **(9)** _____ to spend a lot of money to get just the right look for your cans and bottles.

# Grammar

**3**  Write *T* (true) or *F* (false) next to each sentence.

**1.** My sister, who moved to Florida twelve years ago, stays in touch with old friends by email.

I have more than one sister. _F_

**2.** Cable TV companies that also offer Internet services are very convenient.

All cable TV companies offer Internet services. ____

**3.** My brother who lives in California started his own computer business.

I have more than one brother. ____

**4.** His computer, which is extremely fast, is loaded with computer games.

He has more than one computer. ____

**5.** To turn on the laptop, you should press the round button, which is on the back.

There is more than one round button. ____

**4**  Combine the sentences using a non-defining relative clause to give the extra information. Add a relative pronoun and make any other changes.

**1.** The Olympic Games has become a major business. It is a gathering of the world's best athletes.

The Olympic Games, which is a gathering of the world's best athletes, has become a major business.

**2.** Broadcasting companies pay a lot of money to televise the Olympics. Their profits come from advertising.

_____

**3.** Commercials shown during figure skating events are the most expensive. Figure skating events are very popular.

_____

**4.** Sports equipment companies see the Olympics as a way to show off their products. They pay top athletes to use their equipment.

_____

**5.** Cities from around the world compete for the privilege of hosting the Olympics. These cities usually undergo major construction.

_____

**6.** Participants and spectators contribute to the host city's economy. They come from all over the world.

_____

121

## Listening

**5** 🎧 Play track 57. Listen to the first part of a radio program about eBay, an Internet business. Check (✓) the pictures of the items the speaker mentions.

1. ___   2. ___   3. ___   4. ___

5. ___   6. ___   7. ___

**6** 🎧 Play track 57 again. Fill in the blanks.

1. eBay, _____ _____ _____ by Pierre Omidyar in his California living room, began as a simple meeting place on the Internet, _____ _____ could exchange collectibles.

2. The story goes that Pierre, _____ _____ is a collector, created a website because his girlfriend wanted to trade collectibles on the Internet but had no place to go.

## Pronunciation

**7** 🎧 Play track 59. Notice the way the speaker changes intonation and pauses before and after the non-defining relative clause. In each sentence, underline the two or three words that have the strongest stress.

1. Some <u>credit</u> card companies, which often carry high-<u>interest</u> rates, make enormous <u>profits</u>.

2. My best friend, who works in advertising, earns a huge salary.

3. Osaka, Japan, where I went on business last year, has a spectacular airport.

4. Oprah Winfrey, who is a famous TV talk-show host, is a brilliant businesswoman.

5. Toby Mott, whose business plan was very simple, made a lot of money in a short period of time.

6. Many companies market their products to teenagers, who have a lot of spending power.

7. Mexico City, where you can buy beautiful and original hand-made products, is a shopper's paradise.

8. My friend, who was tired of the cold weather, decided to move to Caracas.

9. Australia, which has become known as a great wine-producing country, produces world-famous wool.

**8** 🎧 Play track 59 again. Listen and repeat.

# Reading

**9** People associate certain products with brands, such as computers and IBM. Which brands do you associate with these products?

athletic shoes     cars     coffee     jeans     software

**10** Read the article. What is the main idea?

   **a.** Advertising persuades us to buy things we don't need.

   **b.** A brand image is very powerful in marketing.

   **c.** Logos represent products.

## Branding: What's in a name?

As consumers, we have all experienced the power of advertising and packaging. Ads tempt us to buy products or services we may or may not need. Clever package designs convince us that a product is trendy, **tasty**, or user-friendly. But branding has even greater **sway** over many of us.

Company logos, like the apple on Macintosh computers, now represent more than just a product, but a lifestyle, an attitude, even an emotional connection. For example, many people buy brand name athletic shoes not because of their quality, but because of their image—it's "cool" to wear them. Even sports celebrities wear them. Why do people pay for brand names in the supermarket, when they can often get the same products for much less, sometimes half the price?

Selling a brand **identity** has become more important than selling the product. Brand names have been around for a long time, but in the past, companies were mainly focused on manufacturing their own products. As mass-produced **goods** became more **uniform**, shoppers couldn't tell different companies' products apart. So corporations spent their **resources** largely on building their brand image.

Do "the best" brands really represent the best quality? Only in the mind of the consumer. For example, in a **ranking** of sixteen small cars, the top quality car was number twelve in sales. In a "taste test," different brands of bottled water were compared. The tasters were blindfolded and didn't know which ones they were tasting. Which one did they judge to have the best taste? Ordinary tap water!

So which brands do you buy, and why?

**11** Read the article again. Write *T* (true) or *F* (false) after each statement.

   **1.** Quality is more important than branding in selling products. _____

   **2.** Brands often represent attitudes and lifestyles. _____

   **3.** Well-known brands usually have the best quality. _____

**12** Find the word in bold that means

   **a.** the same _____   **b.** products _____   **c.** influence _____

# If only . . .

## Vocabulary

**1** Match the words and expressions with their definitions.

**1.** bargain __i__

**2.** clearance sale ____

**3.** haggle ____

**4.** on impulse ____

**5.** refund ____

**6.** shop around ____

**7.** take something back ____

**8.** try clothes on ____

**9.** vendor ____

**a.** check if pants, shirts, etc., fit

**b.** someone who sells things

**c.** return something to a store

**d.** money given back to you if you are not satisfied with the goods or services you have paid for

**e.** a time in which things are priced very cheaply to get rid of them

**f.** following a sudden desire to do something without thinking about the results

**g.** argue about the amount of money you will pay for something

**h.** compare the price and quality of different things before deciding which to buy

**i.** something bought for less than its usual price

**2** Complete the article with the appropriate form of the words and expressions from Exercise 1.

# Tips for the Smart Shopper

- Even though you know your size, always **(1)** ___try clothes on___. The same goes for shoes. It takes only a few minutes—and it's time well spent. Remember that most stores don't allow returns or exchanges on items bought at a **(2)** _____. Play it safe. No matter how little you paid for something, you'll be angry if you can't wear it!

- Save your receipts for at least a month. If you need to **(3)** _____ for whatever reason, it will be easier if you have the receipt. Many stores will not give you a **(4)** _____ without one.

- Don't buy expensive designer goods from street **(5)** _____. If someone tries to sell you a watch for a ridiculously low price, it may seem like a **(6)** _____. Chances are, however, that it's a copy—and not the real thing.

- We've all bought something **(7)** _____ at one time or another. It's human nature, isn't it? We see something and decide we HAVE to have it—whether we need it or can afford it or not. The smart shopper **(8)** _____ for the best deal and doesn't buy without thinking first.

- There are times when it's OK to **(9)** _____. Car dealers, for example, expect to work hard to make a sale—often reducing prices in order to get your business.

# Grammar

**3** Complete the story with the correct form of the verbs in parentheses.

## A Lucky Break!

Taka and Yoko got married last year. But if it **(1)** _hadn't been_ **(be)** for an odd accident, they **(2)** _____ **(meet)**. One evening last year, Taka was in a toy store buying a birthday present for his nephew. A little girl had been trying out some in-line skates. She skated into Taka, who fell and broke his leg. He says, "If the little girl **(3)** _____ **(skate)** into me, I **(4)** _____ **(fall)**. And if I **(5)** _____ **(fall)**, I **(6)** _____ **(break)** my leg. And if I **(7)** _____ **(break)** my leg, I **(8)** _____ **(meet)** Yoko!" Yoko, who was the doctor on duty in the emergency room, said, "If I **(9)** _____ **(have)** the night shift the week of Taka's accident, I **(10)** _____ **(be)** on duty when Taka arrived at the hospital."

**4** Write sentences expressing regret. Begin the sentences with the words in parentheses.

**1.** He didn't listen to our advice. He paid too much. **(He wishes)**

   _He wishes he had listened to our advice._

**2.** I brought my new credit card. I spent too much money. **(If)**

   _____

**3.** We missed the big sale at Better Buys. We didn't get a new CD player. **(If)**

   _____

**4.** She threw away her receipt. The store refused to give her the money back. **(If only)**

   _____

**5.** They weren't patient. They paid too much for their house. **(They wish)**

   _____

**6.** I bought this T-shirt yesterday. It's horrible. **(I wish)**

   _____

**7.** A wonderful company offered me a job. I accepted a different one the day before. **(If only)**

   _____

**8.** I didn't know there was going to be a sale next week. I didn't wait until then to buy Paco's birthday present. **(If)**

   _____

# Listening

**5** 🎧 **Play track 60. Listen to the two roommates talking about shopping. Write *T* (true) or *F* (false) next to each statement.**

Rita . . .

1. would have gone to Abbot's if she had seen the ad. _T_

2. would have saved money if she had bought the coat at Abbot's. ____

3. haggled with the vendor and got a good price. ____

4. tells her friend, "If only you hadn't showed me the ad." ____

5. will probably return the coat. ____

**6** 🎧 **Play track 60 again. Correct the sentences about the conversation.**

1. Rita bought some ~~pants~~ *sweaters* and a coat.

2. The coat is made of wool.

3. Rita bought the coat at a small store.

4. The coat is $90 at Abbot's.

5. Rita paid almost three times more for her coat.

6. Rita thinks she got a good deal.

# Pronunciation

**7** 🎧 **Play track 61. Listen. Notice that the sound /n/ can form a syllable by itself without a vowel sound. Fill in the blanks.**

1. I _didn't_ _see_ the ad.

2. If I'd seen the ad, I _____ _____ bought it from a vendor.

3. I wish I _____ _____ the hat.

4. If I _____ _____ the hat, I _____ _____ felt so stupid!

5. If only I _____ _____ her birthday!

6. If I _____ _____ her birthday, she _____ have _____ upset.

**8** 🎧 **Play track 61 again. Listen and repeat.**

## Reading

**9** Look at the title of the article. What do you think the article will be about?

a. things people buy and lose

b. things people buy and forget they have

c. things people buy that disappoint them

**10** Read the article. What is the main idea?

a. People often buy things that they don't need.

b. People often buy things that they never use.

c. People often buy things that they return to the store.

# Bought and Barely Used

What was the last electronic **gadget** you bought? A scanner? A **state-of-the-art** CD burner to make copies of CDs? Perhaps a Webcam, a video camera that sends images over the Internet? Do you still have it now? Or, do you still use it now? Do you even know where it is?

**Chances are** you don't have it anymore, or if you do, you don't use it and don't even know where you stashed it if you had wanted to use it.

"NIB" or "new in box" refers to those products, **devices**, and gadgets that a buyer couldn't wait to buy, but that inevitably **end up** stuffed into a bottom drawer or hidden away in a closet. Consumers often **acquire** them because they promise to make their lives more fun, efficient, or better. Unfortunately though, in reality, many such gadgets not only are simply too complicated to use but also **fail to fulfill** the buyer's dreams and expectations.

Sandy Fisher, 35, a lawyer in Atlanta, Georgia, is one consumer whose passion for consumer electronics left her closets cluttered with NIBs. Her digital camera came with a user's manual as thick as a Harry Potter book and as **challenging** as an advanced chemistry textbook. Her CD burner, which she bought on a final sale to make copies of photos she takes for her friends, was never actually compatible with her computer. And the exercise equipment she got to help her get into better shape required additional attachments. Unfortunately, by the time she did anything about it, the model she had was no longer being manufactured.

**11** Read the article again. According to the author, which two are reasons a product becomes a NIB?

a. It took too much time to use.

b. It needed additional parts.

c. It was too hard to use.

**12** Find the word or expression in bold that means

a. It's likely that _____

b. small tool or machine _____

c. modern _____

d. be somewhere you didn't plan to be _____

# Positive thinking

## Vocabulary

**1** Complete the sentences with the words in the box.

| ~~bitter~~ | cynical | easygoing | glum | level-headed |
| optimistic | pessimistic | short-tempered | sociable | |

1. A ___bitter___ person feels angry most of the time because of one or more bad past experiences. A _____ person gets angry very easily and quickly.

2. Someone who is _____ sees the glass as half full. A _____ person sees it as half empty.

3. _____ people are not easily worried or annoyed, but that doesn't mean they are always _____—their good nature often causes them to show bad judgment!

4. _____ people usually think it is a fact that their fellow humans don't always have good intentions, and it doesn't make them sad. They're very different from _____ people, who are easily saddened by the world around them.

5. A _____ person will not have problems meeting new people at a party.

**2** Match each quotation with an adjective from Exercise 1. You will not need all of them.

1.
> Why did you do that?
> I told you not to!

___short-tempered___

2.
> I'll meet you at the theater at 8:00, OK? I'm looking forward to meeting your friends. We'll have a great time.

_____

3.
> He's a politician. Of course, he's lying. They always do.

_____

4.
> I keep things to myself. I once shared a secret with a friend and he told several people. I learned my lesson: Don't trust anyone.

_____

5.
> I'm very excited because tomorrow I'm starting at a new job. I'm sure I'm going to do great there.

_____

6.
> I'd never spend money buying a lottery ticket. The chances of winning are close to zero.

_____

# Grammar

**3** Read each pair of sentences. Draw lines to the infinitive or gerund to correctly complete the sentences.

1. a. Do you plan — living
   b. Are you interested in — to live
   in the city?

2. a. We're thinking of — to buy
   b. We hope — buying
   a new car soon.

3. a. He avoids — to work
   b. He expects — working
   very hard.

4. a. She can't help — to love
   b. She seems — loving
   him very much.

5. a. I need — waiting
   b. I can't stand — to wait
   in line to buy tickets.

**4** Complete the conversations with the correct form of the verbs in parentheses.

1. **A:** Are you interested in ___seeing___ (see) a movie tonight?

   **B:** Oh, I avoid _____ (go) out on weekdays. Do you mind _____ (wait) until Saturday?

2. **A:** I'm thinking about _____ (drive) up to Boston this weekend.

   **B:** You seem _____ (spend) a lot of time there. Instead of _____ (go) to Boston, why not plan _____ (stay) here? You and I can hang out together.

3. **A:** Every time I see Jorge, I can't help _____ (wonder) why he always seems so glum.

   **B:** Have you thought of _____ (ask) him? You might help him feel better by _____ (talk) about it.

4. **A:** I'm looking forward to _____ (start) a new semester.

   **B:** Not me. I've enjoyed life without _____ (study) these past few weeks. I'm pretty tired of _____ (be) a student. In fact, I hope _____ (take) a break from school next year.

5. **A:** I'm thinking about _____ (buy) a new computer. Do you have any suggestions?

   **B:** First of all, what do you want _____ (do) with it?

   **A:** Well, I work with graphics, and I also do a lot of photo editing.

   **B:** Then you should count on _____ (spend) some money.

## Listening

**5** 🎧 Play track 62. Listen to five people talking. Circle the answer that correctly completes the sentences.

**Speaker 1**

1. The speaker is **pessimistic** / **optimistic** about the future.

2. He **seems** / **doesn't seem** upset by the crash.

**Speaker 2**

1. The speaker thinks she failed **one** / **all** of her classes.

2. When she sees her grades, she's **disappointed** / **pleasantly surprised**.

**Speaker 3**

1. Sam got his promotion **before** / **after** he was scheduled to receive it.

2. The speaker **trusts** / **doesn't trust** his superiors at work.

**Speaker 4**

1. The speaker talks about **the other person's clothing** / **the weather**.

2. The speaker **knows** / **wants to know** how the other person feels.

**Speaker 5**

1. The speaker mentions **radio** / **television** as a source of news.

2. He probably **expects** / **doesn't expect** things to improve soon.

**6** 🎧 Play track 62 again. Complete the sentences with the words you hear.

1. Nothing _____ _____ go wrong.

2. I guess _____ _____ _____ opening it.

3. They _____ _____ a promotion this year.

4. How _____ _____ going _____ _____?

5. It's _____ _____ and nothing ever changes.

## Pronunciation

**7** 🎧 Play track 63. Listen. Notice the words that are stressed. Underline the stressed words in each sentence.

1. You <u>plan</u> to <u>live</u> to the <u>age</u> of a <u>hundred</u>.

2. You expect to be full of energy.

3. You look forward to retiring.

4. You hope to travel and see lots of new places.

5. You stay home instead of going to the picnic.

6. You're afraid of getting caught in the rain.

**8** 🎧 Play track 63 again. Listen and repeat.

# Reading

**9** **Which one of these statements do you think is true?**

a. Optimists are healthier than pessimists.

b. Pessimists are healthier than optimists.

c. Optimists and pessimists are equally healthy.

**10** **Read the article. Which option is the best title?**

a. Optimism Can't Cure Illness.

b. Optimists Don't Get Sick.

c. Pessimism Can Make You Sick.

**11** **According to the article, what is a possible reason for the difference between optimists' and pessimists' health?**

a. bad habits          b. colds          c. stress

DO YOU HAVE A CHEERFUL, SUNNY disposition and always look on the bright side, or are you a glum pessimist, prepared for the worst? If you're a pessimist, beware: A negative **outlook** over a long period of time can actually make you ill! **Conversely**, an optimistic attitude might keep you healthy, **ward off** some illnesses, and even add years to your life.

Not everyone believes there is a mind-body connection in physical health, but scientific studies indicate there's a link. One study evaluated hundreds of people to determine if their attitudes leaned toward optimism or pessimism. When the same people were examined years later, the optimists had **significantly** fewer illnesses or other health problems. **In fact**, the people in the optimistic group tended to live longer than the pessimists. Recent studies also suggest that pessimists catch more colds than optimists, and their colds tend to be more severe.

What is the reason for this **disparity**? One theory is that pessimists are more likely to feel stressed out. Stress **affects** the body's immune system, which fights off colds and other illnesses. When we experience stress, it lowers our immune defenses.

Negativity and pessimism are difficult personality **traits** to change, so what can you do if you're a pessimist? Use your imagination, for one thing. For example, if you have an important interview coming up, picture yourself answering questions **confidently**. Try to avoid negative thinking by telling yourself that you will succeed, even if you don't completely believe it. Adopting a sunny **outlook** will make you feel better, in more ways than one.

**12** **Read the article again. Write *T* (true) or *F* (false).**

The writer believes that pessimists cannot change their outlook. _____

**13** **Find the word or expression in bold that means**

a. characteristics _____

b. difference _____

c. protect against _____

d. in opposition _____

# Ice Maiden

## Vocabulary

**1** Complete the crossword puzzle.

**Across**

**1** Social or professional position (in relation to other people)

**5** People living together in an organized way with the same laws and similar ways of doing things

**7** Family members who lived and died long ago

**Down**

**2** Ways of doing something that have existed for a long time

**3** Practices shared by a group of people

**4** Members of a family or social group of about the same age

**6** Social group of people of the same race who share beliefs and language and live in a particular area

**8** The ideas, beliefs, and art common to a group of people

Crossword grid with 1 across: s t a t u s

**2** Complete the sentences with the appropriate form of the words in Exercise 1.

**1.** In some ancient ___societies___, women are not allowed to be chiefs.

**2.** It is the _____ in many Asian countries to take off your shoes before entering someone's home.

**3.** Archeologists can often determine what a person's _____ was by the kinds of clothing and possessions they find buried with him.

**4.** The younger _____ often has different views from their older relatives.

**5.** When I travel, I try to go to museums to find out about the _____ of the country I'm in.

**6.** The Amazon rainforest is home to several _____, including the Cabaclos, Maniocs, and Kayapos. These native peoples live in isolation from the outside world.

**7.** *Tet* is an annual celebration during which many Vietnamese families honor their _____ and invite their dead relatives' spirits to share the holiday with them.

**8.** You may think it's strange that we go to the beach every New Year's, but it's an old family _____.

# Grammar

**3** Complete the article using the cues in parentheses to speculate about the past.

## The Nazca Lines

The Nazca lines of Peru are one of the greatest unsolved mysteries in the world. Historians only discovered these amazing lines by flying over the desert. Who (1) _could have made_ (could/make) these lines, which are visible only from the air? What (2) _____ (could/they/be) for?

Many theories have been suggested. One theory is that the Nazca people (3) _____ (might/make) a huge calendar from the lines. Others think that the designs of animals, such as monkeys, birds, and spiders, (4) _____ (might/represent) the stars, which helped the farmers to plant food. Some people believe that the lines were art forms or that the people (5) _____ (could/use) the designs to ask their gods to send rain. The strangest idea of all is that the lines (6) _____ (might/show) aircraft from outer space where to land. It's difficult to prove that this isn't true, of course, but some historians say that extraterrestrials (7) _____ (can't/be) responsible for the lines: Would creatures from outer space have created drawings in the shape of spiders and monkeys?

Most experts are almost certain of one thing, though: The Nazca people, a civilization that lived centuries before the Incas, (8) _____ (must/make) the lines. And if that's true, they (9) _____ (must/have) very sophisticated instruments and equipment.

**4** Write statements with *can't, could, may, might,* or *must* to speculate about the past. Use the words in parentheses to guide you. More than one answer is possible in some cases.

1. He was late for the meeting. Did he miss the train? **(possibly)**

   _He might have missed the train._

2. She brought them yellow flowers. She didn't know that yellow had a negative meaning in some cultures. **(almost certainly not)**

   _____

3. We waited for over an hour. Did they forget our date? **(maybe)**

   _____

4. They didn't take off their shoes before going into the house. Didn't they know anything about Thai customs? **(probably not)**

   _____

5. The archaeologists seemed very excited. Did they find something interesting? **(possibly)**

   _____

6. He didn't come to the boss's party. Didn't he know about it? **(maybe not)**

   _____

# 28

## Listening

**5** ∩ Play track 64. Listen to the two people talk about a TV documentary about the Ice Maiden. Underline the answers that correctly complete the sentences.

1. The archaeologists believe the Ice Maiden's tattoos **were only for decoration** / <u>were pictures that told stories.</u>

2. The woman thinks scientists are similar to **storytellers / detectives**.

3. One reason the archaeologists think the Ice Maiden rode horses was that **they found horses near her / she had tattoos of horses on her legs**.

4. The Ice Maiden was wearing a silk **dress / blouse**.

5. The area where the Ice Maiden was found is **close to / far from** China.

6. It was **unusual / common** for women from tribes in that area to be soldiers.

**6** ∩ Play track 64 again. Which sentence do you hear? Listen and circle *a* or *b*.

1. a. The tattoos might have illustrated stories.
   b. The tattoos must have illustrated stories.

2. a. Scientists can dig things up and figure out how people might have lived.
   b. Scientists can dig things up and figure out how people may have lived.

3. a. They thought she may have ridden horses.
   b. They knew she must have ridden horses.

4. a. It might not have come from the area they lived in.
   b. It can't have come from the area they lived in.

5. a. Their tribe may have traveled long distances.
   b. Their tribe might have traveled long distances.

6. a. She might not have been a warrior.
   b. She must have been a warrior.

## Pronunciation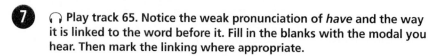

**7** ∩ Play track 65. Notice the weak pronunciation of *have* and the way it is linked to the word before it. Fill in the blanks with the modal you hear. Then mark the linking where appropriate.

1. She __must__ have been someone important.

2. She _____ have been a storyteller.

3. She _____ have been a religious figure.

4. She _____ not have been a warrior.

5. The silk _____ have come from that area.

6. It _____ have come from China.

**8** ∩ Play track 65 again. Listen and repeat.

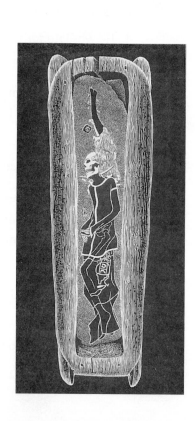

134

# Reading

**9** **Read the title of the article. Guess. Who do you think Oezti was?**

**a.** someone who lived in the Antarctica

**b.** someone who sold ice

**c.** someone who lived thousands of years ago

**10** **Read the article. Check (✔) the statements that are true about Oetzi's life.**

___ **a.** He lived in a mountainous area.

___ **b.** He had a relatively easy life.

___ **c.** He was killed in a battle.

___ **d.** He was a farmer.

___ **e.** He died from a fall after a battle.

## Oetzi the Iceman

One cold September day in 1991, two German tourists made a sensational discovery. Hiking through an Alpine glacier in the Oetz Valley, on the border between Italy and Austria, they strayed from the main path and came across a corpse buried in the ice. Had they just found the missing evidence from an unsolved crime, the body of an unlucky hiker, or something more extraordinary? Experts were called to the scene. They found out that the corpse was well preserved and partially clothed in goatskin leggings and a grass cape, and there was an axe and a bow and arrows lying nearby. It was soon determined that "Oetzi the Iceman," as he came to be known, was over 5,300 years old—the oldest frozen mummy ever found.

The discovery created huge excitement in the scientific world, with international teams of scientists and archaeologists presenting a wide range of contradictory theories on who Oetzi was and how he died.

It has been established that the Iceman was 159 cm tall and 46 years old when he died. He led a rough life: He was arthritic and had suffered numerous injuries and illnesses in the months prior to his death. It was originally assumed that Oetzi had died from a fall or from cold or hunger. But several years ago, an X-ray uncovered an arrowhead stuck in the Iceman's shoulder. This led to speculation that Oetzi was involved in a fight soon before his death, ran into the mountains to escape his attackers, and bled to death from his wounds. Later, additional wounds were found on Oetzi's hand, indicating that he might have tried to defend himself in close hand-to-hand combat.

Scientists continue to analyze Oetzi's remains, which are now housed in a very cold igloo inside a museum in Northern Italy. Their findings provide a glimpse into how people lived and died 5,300 years ago.

**11** **Read the article again. Were the circumstances of Oetzi's death immediately clear to scientists? Find at least two pieces of evidence in the article to support your opinion.**

_____

_____

**12** **In paragraph 1, what expression means _found something by accident_?**

_____

**13** **In paragraph 4, what word means _quick look_?** _____

# Self-Quiz for Units 25–28

## Vocabulary

### UNIT 25

**A** Read the pairs of sentences. Write *S* if the sentences have the same meaning or *D* if the meanings are different.

1. They don't advertise on TV.  They don't tell about their products on TV. __S__
2. Our company is now making a profit.  Our company is now losing money. _____
3. Their items are produced overseas.  Their items are made overseas. _____
4. Did you design a company logo?  Did you come up with a company logo? _____
5. What is the market for this product?  Who do you think will buy this product? _____
6. Today's meeting wasn't planned at all.  We had an improvised meeting. _____

### UNIT 26

**B** Match the words with the definitions.

1. clearance sale __d__
2. refund _____
3. vendor _____
4. on impulse _____
5. bargain _____
6. haggle _____

a. someone who sells things
b. something bought cheaply or for less than its usual price
c. to argue in order to lower the price of something
d. when a store sells items for low prices to sell them quickly
e. money that is given back to you
f. with a sudden desire to do something without thinking about it

### UNIT 27

**C** Circle the word that does <u>not</u> belong in each group.

1. bitter        upset          (cheerful)
2. sociable      friendly       isolated
3. glum          sad            petrified
4. optimistic    pessimistic    positive
5. short-tempered easygoing     stressed out
6. hopeful       cynical        pessimistic

### UNIT 28

**D** Underline the word that completes each sentence.

1. It is a **culture** / <u>tradition</u> / **status** in the U.S. to wear green on St. Patrick's Day.
2. There are only two **customs** / **generations** / **cultures** in most households—parents and their children.
3. My boss has a higher **society** / **status** / **generation** in the company than I do.
4. My great grandmother's **societies** / **cultures** / **ancestors** are from Russia.
5. Each Native American **tribe** / **ancestor** / **custom** has its own traditions.
6. Most Latin American **traditions** / **cultures** / **generations** are very warm and open.

136

# Grammar

## UNIT 25

**A** Complete each sentence with *where*, *which*, *who*, or *whose*.

1. Robert and Katie, ___who___ started out as friends, have been married for three years.

2. Online shopping, _____ is a relatively new idea, has now become very popular.

3. We recently remodeled our basement, _____ I do all of my work.

4. Mozart, _____ music is world famous, is said to have died a poor man.

5. She spoke to her neighbor, _____ is a pharmacist, about the medication.

6. Valentine's Day, _____ began as a religious holiday, is a big money-maker for retailers.

## UNIT 26

**B** Combine the sentences. Begin the new sentence with the words in parentheses.

1. I didn't call Bill last night. I feel bad about it. **(I wish)**
   I wish I had called Bill last night because I feel bad about it.

2. She ate too much chocolate. She got a stomach ache. **(If she)**

3. Buddy was speeding. A police officer gave him a ticket. **(If Buddy)**

4. The couple bought the house without asking a lot of questions. Now they're sorry. **(If only they)**

5. Delia left her wallet at home. She couldn't buy anything. **(If Delia)**

6. Kelly took her friend's bad advice. She made a big mistake. **(Kelly wishes)**

## UNIT 27

**C** Complete each sentence with the infinitive or gerund form of the verb in parentheses.

1. How many people do they expect ___to have___ on opening night? **(have)**

2. The company has been looking forward to _____ its product line. **(expand)**

3. Elvis Presley sang a song called "Can't Help _____ in Love With You." **(fall)**

4. You should help ensure your future by _____ a financial advisor. **(hire)**

5. Would you mind _____ these files in alphabetical order? **(organize)**

6. The president chose _____ the new budget after taking a break. **(present)**

## UNIT 28

**D** Complete each sentence with *may have*, *might have*, *could have*, *can't have*, or *must have* and the correct form of the verbs in parentheses. Some sentences may have more than one possible answer.

Police are investigating a report of a theft. The crime **(1)** _may have occured_ (occur) late last night. There is no evidence of a break in, so the intruder **(2)** _____ (use) a key, or he **(3)** _____ (enter) through an unlocked door. The person **(4)** _____ (be) interested in jewelry, because he didn't touch anything else. But he **(5)** _____ (know) much about jewelry, because he left the most valuable pieces. Police were questioning jewelers in the area, because the thief **(6)** _____ (try) to sell some of the stolen pieces.

# Self-Quiz Answer Key

## UNITS 1–4
### Vocabulary
**Exercise A**
1. O
2. O
3. S
4. S
5. O
6. O

**Exercise B**
1. f
2. a
3. d
4. b
5. e
6. c

**Exercise C**
1. butter
2. onions
3. beer
4. garlic
5. water
6. shrimp

**Exercise D**
1. stuffed animal
2. skateboard
3. jigsaw puzzle
4. cards
5. handheld video game
6. action figure

### Grammar
**Exercise A**
1. already
2. just
3. yet
4. already
5. yet
6. already

**Exercise B**
1. 'll like
2. travel
3. will be
4. like
5. 'll be
6. buy

**Exercise C**
1. a few
2. many
3. a little
4. several
5. many
6. all

**Exercise D**
1. will
2. may/might/could
3. may/might/could
4. may/might/could
5. will
6. may/might/could

## UNITS 5–8
### Vocabulary
**Exercise A**
1. c
2. e
3. f
4. a
5. d
6. b

**Exercise B**
1. invent
2. come up with
3. overcome
4. solve
5. pass
6. achieve

**Exercise C**
1. F
2. F
3. T
4. T
5. T
6. T

**Exercise D**
1. luggage
2. check-in counter
3. security checkpoint
4. gate
5. flight attendant
6. baggage claim

### Grammar
**Exercise A**
1. Can I look at your calendar?
2. May I borrow your car?
3. Could I use your phone?
4. Would you mind if I sit here?
5. Do you mind if I order a drink?
6. Is it OK if I arrive a little late?

**Exercise B**
1. has won
2. have been eating
3. has written
4. has not received
5. has been speaking
6. have been working

**Exercise C**
1. in case
2. so that
3. in order to
4. so that
5. in case
6. for

**Exercise D**
1. had already eaten; didn't order
2. checked; had left
3. didn't enjoy; had seen
4. read; had already heard
5. were; hadn't eaten
6. knew; had made

## UNITS 9–12
### Vocabulary
**Exercise A**
1. e
2. f
3. a
4. c
5. d
6. b

**Exercise B**
1. gotten better
2. deteriorated
3. climbed
4. dropped
5. worsened
6. climbing

**Exercise C**
1. long-term goal
2. promotion
3. reference
4. strength
5. prospect
6. qualifications

**Exercise D**
1. previously
2. afterwards
3. at the same time, simultaneously
4. every time, whenever
5. Whenever
6. subsequently, afterwards

### Grammar
**Exercise A**
1. Laura told her husband that they needed to get milk on the way home.
2. The reporter said that the storm would get worse before it got better.
3. Ursula said that she really wanted to go with us, but she couldn't.
4. Mr. Greer told his daughter that he would read her a story after she got in bed.
5. James said that he had seen the movie earlier this week.
6. The spokesperson told the press that the governor will have made a decision in the morning.

**Exercise B**
1. will have traveled
2. will begin
3. will discover
4. will have gotten used to
5. will have become
6. will remain

**Exercise C**
1. The tourist asked where the opera house was.
2. The customer wanted to know what time the store opened.
3. He wanted me to tell him if I had experience in sales.
4. They wanted to know whether we had enjoyed ourselves.
5. She wanted me to tell her how much I had paid for the jacket.
6. He asked her whether she would be able to make it to the party tonight.

**Exercise D**
1. didn't recognize
2. hadn't seen
3. were talking
4. realized
5. had lived
6. had been talking

# UNITS 13–16
## Vocabulary
**Exercise A**
1. S
2. D
3. S
4. S
5. S
6. D

**Exercise B**
1. leisure
2. take a long
3. By the
4. a waste of
5. a matter of
6. in

**Exercise C**
1. complain
2. confide in
3. gossip
4. talk behind their back
5. make small talk
6. brags

**Exercise D**
1. fashionable
2. influential
3. sensational
4. trendy
5. popular
6. famous

## Grammar
**Exercise A**
1. were; would accept
2. wasn't; would enjoy
3. would look; painted
4. would/do; won
5. trained; would be
6. wouldn't feel; planned

**Exercise B**
1. Although I left work early, I was late for dinner.
2. Despite the expense, she always visits her

sister at least once a year.
3. In spite of not knowing a lot of Spanish, he moved to Bolivia last year.
4. Despite not liking heights, she doesn't mind flying.
5. Although there is a lot of traffic, the commute usually takes about 45 minutes.
6. Maria goes shopping a lot. However, she doesn't spend a lot of money.

**Exercise C**
1. do you
2. can't he
3. did you
4. will he
5. weren't you
6. haven't they

**Exercise D**
1. was elected
2. were introduced
3. are interviewed
4. is imported
5. are consumed
6. was entertained

# UNITS 17–20
## Vocabulary
**Exercise A**
1. cheese
2. bake
3. meat
4. roast beef
5. sandwich
6. ice cream

**Exercise B**
1. prisoners
2. cell
3. authorities
4. supervision
5. privilege
6. guard

**Exercise C**
1. f
2. d
3. e
4. b

5. a
6. c

**Exercise D**
1. smells like
2. feels
3. tastes
4. looks like
5. sounds like
6. feels like

## Grammar
**Exercise A**
1. eating
2. running
3. reading
4. to get
5. to fly
6. to make

**Exercise B**
1. not allowed to
2. made
3. don't let
4. didn't make
5. let
6. was not allowed to

**Exercise C**
1. has been studying
2. had gone
3. had been talking
4. had been based
5. hadn't read
6. hadn't been dating

**Exercise D**
1. where
2. that
3. who
4. that
5. whose
6. which

# UNITS 21–24
## Vocabulary
**Exercise A**
1. b
2. d
3. e
4. f
5. a
6. c

**Exercise B**
1. contact
2. an appointment

3. an agreement
4. risks
5. a deal
6. business cards

**Exercise C**
1. get away with
2. look up to
3. think over
4. count on
5. look forward to
6. pick on

**Exercise D**
1. delivered
2. do
3. cater
4. fix
5. organize
6. serve

## Grammar
**Exercise A**
1. anything
2. Everything
3. No one
4. anyone
5. Everyone
6. something

**Exercise B**
1. is; 'll/will give
2. take; 'll/will get
3. would make; listened
4. were; would take
5. would love; worked
6. buy; 'll/will take

**Exercise C**
1. figure it out
2. picking on her younger brother
3. make up things
4. bringing her up
5. count on their parents
6. think over the options

**Exercise D**
1. have the car washed
2. do the cooking myself
3. having the party catered
4. washing the dishes herself
5. have your packages delivered
6. cut my hair myself

# UNITS 25–28

## Vocabulary

### Exercise A
1. S
2. D
3. S
4. S
5. S
6. S

### Exercise B
1. d
2. e
3. a
4. f
5. b
6. c

### Exercise C
1. cheerful
2. isolated
3. petrified
4. pessimistic
5. easygoing
6. hopeful

### Exercise D
1. tradition
2. generations
3. status
4. ancestors
5. tribe
6. cultures

## Grammar

### Exercise A
1. who
2. which
3. where
4. whose
5. who
6. which

### Exercise B
1. I wish I had called Bill last night because I feel bad about it.
2. If she hadn't eaten too much chocolate, she wouldn't have gotten a stomachache.
3. If Buddy hadn't been speeding, a police officer wouldn't have given him a ticket.
4. If only they had asked a lot of questions when they bought the house, they wouldn't be sorry now.
5. If Delia hadn't left her wallet at home, she could have bought something.
6. Kelly wishes she hadn't taken her friend's bad advice and made a big mistake.

### Exercise C
1. to have
2. expanding
3. Falling
4. hiring
5. organizing
6. to present

### Exercise D
1. may have happened
2. may/might/could have used
3. may/might/could have entered
4. must have been
5. can't have known
6. may/might/could have tried

# WorldView 4 Student Audio CD

| TRACK | WORKBOOK PAGE | | ACTIVITY |
|---|---|---|---|
| 1 | | | Audio Program Introduction |
| 2 | 14 | Unit 1 | Listening |
| 3 | 14 | Unit 1 | Pronunciation |
| 4 | 18 | Unit 2 | Pronunciation |
| 5 | 18 | Unit 2 | Listening |
| 6 | 22 | Unit 3 | Listening |
| 7 | 22 | Unit 3 | Pronunciation |
| 8 | 26 | Unit 4 | Listening |
| 9 | 26 | Unit 4 | Pronunciation |
| 10 | 32 | Unit 5 | Listening |
| 11 | 32 | Unit 5 | Pronunciation |
| 12 | | Unit 5 | Pronunciation |
| 13 | | Unit 5 | Pronunciation |
| 14 | 36 | Unit 6 | Listening |
| 15 | 36 | Unit 6 | Pronunciation |
| 16 | 40 | Unit 7 | Listening |
| 17 | | Unit 7 | Pronunciation |
| 18 | 44 | Unit 8 | Listening |
| 19 | 44 | Unit 8 | Pronunciation |
| 20 | 50 | Unit 9 | Listening |
| 21 | | Unit 9 | Pronunciation |
| 22 | 54 | Unit 10 | Listening |
| 23 | 54 | Unit 10 | Pronunciation |
| 24 | 58 | Unit 11 | Listening |
| 25 | 58 | Unit 11 | Pronunciation |
| 26 | 62 | Unit 12 | Listening |
| 27 | | Unit 12 | Pronunciation |
| 28 | 62 | Unit 12 | Pronunciation |
| 29 | 68 | Unit 13 | Listening |
| 30 | 68 | Unit 13 | Pronunciation |
| 31 | 72 | Unit 14 | Listening |
| 32 | 72 | Unit 14 | Pronunciation |
| 33 | 76 | Unit 15 | Listening |
| 34 | | Unit 15 | Pronunciation |
| 35 | 76 | Unit 15 | Pronunciation |
| 36 | 80 | Unit 16 | Pronunciation |
| 37 | 80 | Unit 16 | Listening |
| 38 | | Unit 17 | Pronunciation |
| 39 | | Unit 17 | Pronunciation |
| 40 | 86 | Unit 17 | Listening |
| 41 | 90 | Unit 18 | Listening |
| 42 | 90 | Unit 18 | Pronunciation |
| 43 | 94 | Unit 19 | Listening |
| 44 | 94 | Unit 19 | Pronunciation |
| 45 | 98 | Unit 20 | Listening |
| 46 | 98 | Unit 20 | Pronunciation |
| 47 | | Unit 20 | Pronunciation |
| 48 | 104 | Unit 21 | Listening |
| 49 | 104 | Unit 21 | Pronunciation |
| 50 | 108 | Unit 22 | Listening |
| 51 | 108 | Unit 22 | Pronunciation |
| 52 | 112 | Unit 23 | Listening |
| 53 | 112 | Unit 23 | Pronunciation |
| 54 | 116 | Unit 24 | Listening |
| 55 | | Unit 24 | Pronunciation |
| 56 | 116 | Unit 24 | Pronunciation |
| 57 | 122 | Unit 25 | Listening |
| 58 | | Unit 25 | Pronunciation |
| 59 | 122 | Unit 25 | Pronunciation |
| 60 | 126 | Unit 26 | Listening |
| 61 | 126 | Unit 26 | Pronunciation |
| 62 | 130 | Unit 27 | Listening |
| 63 | 130 | Unit 27 | Pronunciation |
| 64 | 134 | Unit 28 | Listening |
| 65 | 134 | Unit 28 | Pronunciation |
| 66 | 40 | Unit 7 | Extra Pronunciation Practice |
| 67 | 50 | Unit 9 | Extra Pronunciation Practice |
| 68 | 50 | Unit 9 | Extra Pronunciation Practice |
| 69 | 86 | Unit 17 | Extra Pronunciation Practice |